QUESTIONS OF SCIENCE

Questions of Science

Exploring the Interaction between Science and Faith

ANDREW BARTON

KINGSWAY PUBLICATIONS
EASTBOURNE

ISBN 0 85476 779 7

Published by
KINGSWAY PUBLICATIONS
Lottbridge Drove, Eastbourne, BN23 6NT, England.
E-mail: books@kingsway.co.uk

Designed and produced for the publishers by
Bookprint Creative Services, P.O. Box 827, BN21 3YJ, England.
Printed in Great Britain.

Contents

Acknowledgements

My thanks go to Richard Herkes, publishing director of Kingsway, who suggested the format and the scope of this book. He has been a constant encouragement throughout its production. I am conscious that I could not take up all the suggestions of reviewing editors (especially the Revd Derek Williams) and friends who read the manuscript as it developed. Science, like faith, is a subject that is constantly being explored, and new insights are always being discovered and sometimes rediscovered. Any shortcomings of this book therefore are solely mine and not theirs. The difficulty is that I had been asked to write a single book and not a series.

All writers can look back to those who inspired them. Consequently, my thanks go also to Michael Green and John Polkinghorne, two Christian teachers from whom I have been privileged to learn in the past. I hope that I build on their solid foundations.

Foreword

The telephone message simply asked whether I was available to do a primary school assembly. I didn't realise what saying 'yes' would mean! I later found out that the school had asked its 7- to 11-year-olds to come up with the most difficult questions they could think of about God, science and the universe. Then all the questions were collected and a top ten drawn up. My job, for some strange reason, was to go into school and give the answers!

As I walked into the hall in front of 300 children I turned to the Head and said, 'You want me to do five or ten minutes as part of the assembly I suppose?' She replied that in fact lessons had been cancelled and I had at least forty-five minutes. This came as quite a shock and I realised that forty-five minutes without visual aids to 300 children was somewhat beyond me. I shouldn't have worried. After an attempt at their first question, I asked whether anyone had anything else for me to answer. Twenty hands shot up. For the next hour or so (as the children refused to go out for their break) we explored everything from evolution to miracles, from black holes to Big Bang.

My eyes were opened by that experience. First, to the need that people of all ages and backgrounds have to ask questions: I have had similar experiences in a university lecture theatre and at a nursing home for the elderly. Christians are often not very good at allowing people the opportunity to ask questions: perhaps we underestimate the number of questions that people have, or perhaps we are afraid of what they might ask. Yet it was in responding to people's questions that Jesus revealed the truth. After all, if Thomas had not questioned Jesus, Jesus would not have responded with 'I am the way, the truth and the life.'

Second, my eyes were opened to the depth of the questions that people need to ask. The questions the children had, although in a slightly different language, were the fundamental questions of existence posed by scientists, theologians and philosophers across the centuries. The children also showed a great appreciation of science, far more developed than many adult audiences.

Third, the fact that they were reduced to asking me, showed the need to find straightforward answers to some of those questions. They may be interested in whether God and science can be held together in the origin of the universe, but may not want to plough through endless scientific and philosophical books for an answer.

I wish I had read this book in preparation for that assembly. Andrew Barton writes as a scientist and a theologian who is fascinated with the questions: some that have been put to him, but also some that he himself has asked. He writes with humility yet with a refreshing confidence in Christianity's ability to relate to the modern world; he treats the need to ask questions seriously; he responds to questions with depth and detail. And he gives answers in an accessible way.

This is a book that highlights the questions we have all wanted to ask. Those who are already Christians will be challenged by the questions as well as some of the answers. Those who are thinking about the Christian faith will be able to see that, although Christianity does not promise simple solutions to every problem, it has relevant and convincing things to say about the important issues of today.

Whether the questions are from an assembly of 7- to 11-year-olds or are from professional scientists, this book provides answers of integrity and conviction. It highlights many of the questions that I have asked and continue to ask as an astrophysicist and theologian. In addition, it has helped me find clearer answers.

David Wilkinson

Preface

Does faith have any sort of place in a scientific world? Are religious beliefs just quaint anachronisms today akin to believing in Santa Claus? For most of the last two centuries religions have retreated in the face of a scientific rationality that has taken over the world. General knowledge about the Christian faith is so low in the Western world that most people have little or no idea of the gospel message that Jesus Christ can be their living Saviour and Lord. Today even the words of hymns that once might have been remembered from school provoke little response. In this age of science and technology you will get more response from talking about web sites than about worship songs.

Christians may be tempted to despair at this lamentable state of affairs, but it need not be so. Our world is still in great spiritual need. The gospel is not only about a life-changing personal experience but also about a message that is meant to renew the whole of the world. To this end we are bidden by Jesus Christ to proclaim it into every area of life, and to bring God onto every agenda.

The book of Acts tells us of St Paul trying to bring God onto the agenda at Athens. In Acts chapter 17 he links their idea about an unknown god (to whom they had built an altar) with the God whom he had met in Jesus Christ. Paul connects with the mindset of his audience and makes them think about their faith. The citizens of Athens had many gods, but he challenges them to consider what this unknown god might be like. This is the skill of apologetic – not apologising, but vindicating and commending. The New Testament records that Paul did it with some success.

Many people today acknowledge this unknown god. In surveys, about two-thirds still say they believe in God. Some 40 per cent of practising scientists in a 1997 American survey said they did too – virtually the same percentage as in a survey of 1916! Yet to many people their god is in practice non-viable because he is an amalgam: a divinity constructed mostly from personal superstition, different religions or nostalgic longings. God is in reality unknown because faith and life are disconnected. In the same survey 60 per cent of scientists today didn't want immortality, whereas in 1916 75 per cent did![1] Clearly many scientists, like ordinary people, are confused about who the God of the Bible is and what he can do. They do not see him as creator, redeemer and guide in life, but as a remote figure inhabiting a strange, private world of half-remembered Bible stories and beliefs.

Christians need to be equipped to draw people into thinking about God, just as St Paul did. This requires a clear understanding of how twentieth-century science has opened up insights into the meaning and mystery of life, and how it can reinforce rather than discredit faith. Old antagonisms from previous centuries have begun to

be replaced by newer, deeper insights. As the new millennium dawns, people are still fascinated by the bigger
questions that science throws up, be it the nature of the
universe or whether there is any meaning to existence.
They ask questions about this unknown god just as they
did in Paul's day. Very often Christians find it difficult
to answer them, because enquirers never say, 'What
must I do to be saved?' but rather, 'The universe is
mind-numbingly big. Surely we are just insignificant
accidents?'

This book looks at fifty such questions and attempts to
answer them from a Christian perspective. The answers
are meant to try to dispel the idea that science and faith
are always at loggerheads, and they assert that belief in
God is credible today. Indeed, faith can challenge science
about its basis of authority and its presuppositions, and
can provide guidance about how we should live our
lives in a scientific age. The questions are not exhaustive,
but they are the sort of questions that people have asked
me as a former researcher in the physical sciences at
Oxford University. They may not be quite your answers,
and some will demonstrate that science isn't always an
easy subject to grasp, but I hope they'll be a good start
for you to frame yours. The answers aim to be like St
Paul's to the people of Athens. They are intended to
show God to others, or at the very least to suggest that
the Christian faith is one that can be held with integrity
in the modern scientific world.

A guiding verse in this whole enterprise is John 1:3,
'Through him [Jesus] all things were made; without him
nothing was made that has been made.' This is God's
world created through his word, and we should expect
that the Scriptures, God's word, will not conflict with
our discoveries in nature. This does not mean that they

will always be readily harmonised, but it does give us confidence that there is an underlying divine rationale. It is a rationale that underlies both science and the Christian faith, and it seeks and finds genuine truth. The universe makes sense because it is the product of a good God's love.

Finally, this book is not meant to be read steadily from start to finish. It is for browsing through – though preferably not in bookshops! I have tried to ensure that each answer doesn't rely on another. Cross-links are given where appropriate and there is a glossary (a jargon buster!) at the end, defining obscure scientific or philosophical words that you will find underlined in the text.

Andrew Barton
Spring 1999

Note: <u>underlined</u> words are explained more fully in the Glossary at the back of the book.

BACK TO BASICS
What science and religion are all about

1. Science is about facts whereas religion is about opinion or feelings. I prefer facts myself. Don't you?

'Now, what I want is facts . . . facts alone are wanted in life.' So said schoolmaster Mr Gradgrind in Charles Dickens' novel *Hard Times*. His words have been echoed many times during this century of science. If we have the facts about something or someone, we are confident that we know all about them. Facts are the building-blocks of a modern age that collects information just like a squirrel hoards nuts.

Science is brimming with facts. Yet facts themselves do not constitute science, just as a supermarket trolley full of food is not a meal. Facts are the means by which we build a coherent framework for understanding the world. Yet as this scientific framework has developed, it has come into conflict with another framework for understanding the world: that of religion. And when it has, science has often come up with explanations for events that have seemed to contradict religious insight, from explaining the causes of rainbows to the parting of the Red Sea. The result has been that faith has retreated from the real world in the face of an apparently all-encompassing means of deciding what is true.

In science, facts are gained when scientists perform experiments. Yet this practice came late into civilisation, beginning with pioneers such as Galileo in the early seventeenth century. Ancient peoples such as the Greeks, the Romans and the Chinese made many observations in the world, but they did not conduct experiments to

17

find out more. Today, by contrast, science is rooted in the laboratory, not in the library. Yet the common understanding of how science is done is often distorted. We imagine that the boffin goes into his or her laboratory each day, and devises some new experiment that will discover an exciting fact to push back the frontiers of knowledge. In practice, it is rarely like this, for a number of reasons.

First, few experiments are done in isolation. There will already be a history of research done within a part of the scientific community that has been studying particular phenomena. Experiments will have been done in the past that created models or scenarios to explain the results. Such insights then suggest further experiments that attempt to explore and expand particular models.

Hence, facts in science have a value only as interpreted facts; that is, they only make sense in relation to some scientifically consistent model. These models change and develop as we learn and experiment more. Facts are not value-free. Our question assumes that you can draw a clear line between fact and opinion, but this is not true either in science or in religion. For example, when Christians pray for someone and the person recovers, they explain the outcome by saying that the world is the product of a loving God who wants the best for his people (see also Question 39). Facts need interpretation.

$$E = MC^2$$

Facts only have value as interpreted facts.

Secondly, scientific facts require corroboration. If other research groups around the world cannot reproduce novel experimental results, then they are unlikely to influence scientific theories. Most scientists are highly conservative and they are unwilling to give much time to the unexpected unless they have good supporting evidence, especially if the results suggest they need to make radical changes to their understanding. Scientific worldviews, or <u>paradigms,</u> take a lot of shifting. Similarly, Christians who proclaim novel ideas in the face of biblical truths are unlikely to receive unconditional acceptance.

In practice both science and a major religion such as Christianity operate in a similar fashion. Religious ideas are formed and accepted by groups of believers, who may also be scattered around the world. Indeed, it is the local and unacknowledged deviation that defines a sect. Faith is not about believing what you know is untrue (as cynics frequently suggest); rather it is recognising and adhering to a set of commonly held beliefs as assured facts (see Question 2). Such sets of beliefs must be consistent within themselves to be able to stand up to collective scrutiny. In holding them, the community is necessarily conservative to change. While scientists look back to authoritative experimenters setting the foundations of science, Christians look to the authority of the Bible witnesses and their openness to the consistent revelation of God in Christ.

Therefore the idea that faith is just based on individual opinion is not present in the major world religions. One of the past errors in Western Protestant Christianity has been to over-emphasise the individual's personal beliefs. This was a predictable reaction to overbearing ecclesiastical authority, but its legacy in this <u>postmodern</u> world is a denial of the link between fact and opinion. If you want to define both science and religion, then characterising one as fact-based and the other as opinion-based isn't really possible.

—————————$E=MC^2$—————————

The idea that faith is just based on individual opinion
is not present in the major world religions.

Now, of course, it is perfectly possible for us to be consistent in what we believe yet also to be entirely mistaken. Paradigms can be like ruts in a country road taking us in the wrong direction. It is frequently the observations in science that haven't fitted into existing models that have led to great changes in scientific thought (see, for example, Questions 16–18). Such shifts in understanding, paradigm shifts, are what enable modern science to develop. Revolutionary change is as much a part of religious insight as of scientific discovery. The fact of the existence, death and resurrection of Jesus led to a paradigm shift that both revolutionised and deepened our knowledge of what God is like.

Science and religion do differ in some aspects, however. Jesus' words 'Follow me' give to faith a personal dimension that impersonal science does not have. Indeed the scientist is often characterised as being socially inept, because this element of personal involvement is absent. To know God requires more than the accumulation of facts and the formation of ideas about him. It requires a relationship.

—————————$E=MC^2$—————————

Jesus' words 'Follow me' give to faith a personal
dimension that impersonal science does not have.

Many people think that science and religion are at loggerheads today. Frequently this idea is promoted in the media because arguments make better news than agreements. Yet the polemic continues only on the fringes, where a few scientists take a deliberately atheistic standpoint. In many areas of science recently, there has begun to be much exploration and agreement.

Both science and religion seek to comprehend something of the world in which we live. They assume that the universe is understandable, that what we discover will always have meaning (see also Question 8). Albert Einstein, who often talked about God but seemed to use his name as shorthand for the laws of nature, once said, 'The most unintelligible thing about the universe is that it is intelligible.' Beyond that point of understanding scientists venture into a world of faith.

Sum-up

- Both science and religious belief are concerned with facts and opinions; they both rely on evidence. Facts have value only when they are interpreted.

- Both science and religion make their interpretation in the context of a community, not in isolation.

- Both are open to change provided by new revelations about the way things are.

- Both realise the world around makes sense, and want to ask why it does.

2. Science can never be completely sure about anything, whereas religions often claim to possess absolute truth. Which is right?

How often are you 100 per cent sure of anything in life? The dawn of the new millennium will be characterised by all sorts of uncertainty: economic, ecological, moral and political. Even René Descartes' philosophical starting point, 'I think therefore I am', is open to question if we see our minds as illusions created by our brains to keep us feeling as if we are in control (see Question 31). Brains themselves may be at the mercy of our <u>genes</u> (see Question 28)! Is everything relative, then – even truth? Can both science and religion be of help before we reach out for the bottle of pills to end all our anxieties?

It is correct to say that science doesn't prove things. Only a limited number of experiments can ever be done to see if a proposition is true, and so eventually we have to use our judgement based on experience to reach a conclusion. Hence science is always reasoning from the particular to the general, a method known as <u>induction</u>. Philosopher Karl Popper pointed out that the statements of scientists are not provable, but they can be found to be false at any point.

$$E = MC^2$$

It is correct to say that science doesn't prove things.

Let us suppose we have a new scientific theory. Certain observations go in the theory's favour: when it is consistent with previous ideas; when it predicts unknown results that can be verified; and to some extent how reasonable or likely the theory seems. The last is a matter of experience. Deductions that arise from the theory help it to stand or fall in the scientific community (see Question 1). Science works by using <u>inductive</u> and <u>deductive</u> methods to explain what we see around us. It is <u>empirical</u>, yes, but not just experimental. It relies on researchers' skills of intuition and judgement, and when these are correctly directed it is fair to say that a theory is established beyond reasonable doubt. Science can give explanations that are 'true' in the sense that theory and experiment combine to give a high level of probability.

Some Christian thinkers use this idea of falsifiability as a stick to beat science with. 'You can't prove scientific theories are true,' they say, 'whereas religions are about absolute truths.' In the twentieth century Christian theologians such as Karl Barth have suggested that because of our sinful nature our human insights are always flawed. Now if we recognise that we live without God's absolute perspective, Barth is undoubtedly correct. Truth is undoubtedly provisional to some extent, framed as it is within finite human minds. Scientific theories are often described as hypotheses, which reinforces their lack of absoluteness. Yet it should not be thought that science can never converge upon, nor ever reach the destination of, establishing absolute truth. Both science and Christianity do say that they are closing in upon what is true. But truth needs to be peppered with humility whenever it is proposed. Religious insight does this through statements of faith; science through falsifiability.

If truth is always measured, this does not, however, imply that everything is relative, for new truths usually illuminate past insights more clearly. Revolutions may occur, but much stays the same. For science this is seen through established reliable laws; for Christianity it is by faith in the God who is unchanging (Malachi 3:6).

But while many scientists believe they can provide us with reliable hypotheses, some scientists claim much more. They say that there is no truth but scientific truth. They follow philosophers called positivists, who say that only insights gained by scientific experiments have any meaning, whereas those derived from metaphysics (which explores the nature of ultimate reality) are inherently invalid.

Science then becomes the sole method of deciding truth and the only relevant means of discovery. It becomes a sort of modern 'religion' in itself and the object of worship. This is often termed scientism. Scientism is science separated from society. Science does answer certain questions very well, but this does not mean that these are the only questions worth asking (see Question 7). To assert this is to make a metaphysical claim in itself, and aggressive atheist scientists riding on the scientific bandwagon often do it. Moral values, beauty and love are among the qualities that science cannot pronounce on, but that doesn't mean that they are illusions. Whenever people have suggested that all there was to know about a subject had been discovered, they have always been proved to be wrong.

$$E=MC^2$$

Science does answer certain questions very well, but this does not mean that these are the only questions worth asking. To assert this is to make a metaphysical claim in itself.

By contrast, religion widens the picture and searches for the answers to greater truths from the top down (from the complex to the simple) rather than as science does from the bottom up (from the simple to the more complex). Christian faith derives from a relationship that trusts in a God who has proved faithful in the past (Deuteronomy 7:9). Both approaches can be describing the same set of circumstances but from different vantage points. Former Professor of Mathematical Physics at Cambridge University, and now Anglican priest, Sir John Polkinghorne, described them as 'cousins under the skin'.

Scientists believe that their way of describing and explaining the nature of reality is basically correct. Their findings are often unexpected so that what is discovered appears to be more than the construction of the human mind. So, too, the assertions of faith make more of the world than the human mind often imagines. In creation and in the Bible, God's work and his word are far richer than our limited minds can fathom.

Yet if good science and good religion are not absolutist in their form, neither are they completely relative either. The laws which science frames, and the claims believers make, are not just matters of personal taste (see Question 10). Gravity, for example, works on anyone who might jump off a cliff whether they choose to believe in it or not! Religions rarely say that their beliefs are true only insofar as a person believes them.

Science and the Christian faith both trust that the universe favours the <u>critical realist</u>. Models, metaphors and theories are the stock in trade of people who seek a deeper understanding of what is going on, and they will be reliable because God as creator is reliable. No human understanding is going to be complete and all-encompassing. As St Paul reminds us in 1 Corinthians 13:12, 'Now we see but a poor reflection as in a mirror; then we shall see face to face. Now I know in part; then I shall know fully, even as I am fully known.' A deeper relationship with God and a deeper understanding of the world's working both require time and effort. Revelation of the mysteries of the universe and the revelation of God do not come overnight, but require us to recognise our fallibility.

$$E = MC^2$$

Models, metaphors and theories are the stock in trade of people who seek a deeper understanding of what is going on.

Sum-up

- Experimental science speculates from the particular to the general, so is always open to its theories being found to be false.

- Science should not be confused with the absolutist and metaphysical claims of scientism.

- Science and religion are 'cousins under the skin'. They strive towards absolute truths, but should recognise human fallibility.

3. How on earth can a scientist be a Christian?

If science has been guilty of one sin in the twentieth century it is in becoming the gadget-monger to a rudderless civilisation. The horrors of nuclear conflict, and more recently the consequences of environmental pollution seen in global warming, illustrate the absence in society of a clear moral framework for the application of science. The pursuit of knowledge and its technological applications have caused more carnage and ecological damage in the twentieth century than all the religious wars ever fought (see Question 15).

Recently this has begun to change. Research into the earliest moments of life has led people to ask ethical questions that currently restrict what science may explore, such as human genetic manipulation (see Question 43). This recognises that although God gives us dominion over nature, people created in his image are not given *carte blanche* to do what he would forbid.

$$E=MC^2$$

Although God gives us dominion over nature, people created in his image are not given *carte blanche* to do what he would forbid.

Unless scientists are determined to be totally divorced from social life (and science can never be that) and ignore possible consequences, ethical issues will inevitably impinge on their work. The days when the first British commercial nuclear reactor at Windscale had a filter placed on the exhaust gas stack only by chance (because the Atomic Energy Authority Director had noticed one on his visit to an American reactor) are thankfully long passed. If only because funds are limited and because of media interest, scientists must interact with society to justify their research.

In doing so they inevitably come up against the competing philosophies and theologies of the world. Often because science students specialise early in their education, they lack wisdom to discern between such ideas. The worship of science, that has a wonder of its own, wins out by default. Its authority rests on its predictive abilities and technological power, and it becomes the only real basis of its claim to make value judgements. The claims of religions such as Christianity, in contrast, are often feebly understood, a scientist's knowledge often barely going beyond that of an eight-year-old in Sunday school.

So the British evolutionary biologist Richard Dawkins could suggest in *The Independent* in 1992 that 'Faith is the great cop-out, the great excuse to evade the need to think and evaluate evidence'. Of course it isn't, and the Bible never defines faith in that way. Such a statement goes far beyond the conclusions that science can draw. The life of a Mother Teresa could hardly be taken as evidence of a cop-out, whereas that of an ivory tower scientist might popularly be seen as that! Mother Teresa and countless others have responded to what theologian Francis Schaeffer called the 'brute facts' of the Christian faith. They evaluated the evidence of the life, teachings, death and resurrection of Jesus, the carpenter from Nazareth, and acted upon them.

Faith, then, is not ignoring the evidence but it is the

consequence of evaluating it in a scientific-like manner and then entrusting oneself to God (see also Question 49). Such a faith can provide the foundation for an ethical approach to science that gives a proper basis to the existence of values in creation, and acknowledges the God who designed and upholds the universe they describe.

---------$E=MC^2$----------

Faith, then, is not ignoring the evidence but it is the consequence of evaluating it in a scientific-like manner and then entrusting oneself to God.

Science is about measurement, and God is beyond measurement. Science is concerned with what can be seen, and God cannot be seen. The Old Testament makes that very clear: 'Truly you are a God who hides himself, O God and Saviour of Israel' (Isaiah 45:15). Isaiah was also under no illusion as to the reason: 'Your iniquities have separated you from your God; your sins have hidden his face from you' (Isaiah 59:2). Such texts serve to illustrate the dimension of relationship that was forged with this God of Abraham, Isaac and Jacob; the God who wanted to be known by creatures to whom he had given the capacity to know him. Those names indicate a continuing relationship in history between God and human beings, which theologians call a salvation history. Like all relationships, one with God is not about measurement but about commitment. If we had concrete proof of God's existence, compulsion to believe in him would replace a freely given response.

In times of desperation many people call on the God who is hidden from their sight. Their cry is echoed in Isaiah 64:1: 'Oh, that you would rend the heavens and come down, that the mountains would tremble before you!' The Christian message is that in Christ Jesus God did come down. The disciples, who were fiercely mono-theist Jews, were compelled to suggest this, not by preconceived dogma, but by meeting Jesus and listening to his teaching, and above all by the evidence of his res-urrection (see Romans 1:4 and Question 41).

$$E = MC^2$$

Like all relationships, one with God is not about measurement but about commitment.

A scientist who is a Christian is no less interested in the 'brute facts' of the world. Sadly, people are often antagonistic to scientists today because they have an instinctive desire to retain mystery in their lives. And science seems to be about blowing that mystery apart. This is why books on New Age topics and paganism flourish. People are not discerning when it comes to mystery. Any old mystery will do, and often it is igno-rance in disguise, or it is about being content with easy, shallow solutions. This is sadly often what deters scien-tists from the Christian faith. However, the real mystery is found in demystifying the world. Because it seems, in this created universe, that when you explain a mystery there is always a deeper one underneath. The elegance, the subtlety and the harmony of the universe cannot but awe a scientist, and awe elicits deeper <u>metaphysical</u> questions that are answered by Christianity.

If a scientist wishes to evaluate the evidence, however unusual the conclusions may be or however uncomfort-able to live with, he or she will be drawn to see the lives of countless people who have been changed by an encounter with this man Jesus. His words echo down the centuries like no other. They are life-changing and have provided a new direction for those in many countries in many centuries. His claims are worth a great deal of careful consideration.

Sum-up

● Science rarely confines itself to pure research; applications providing new technology are almost inevitable. Its proponents sometimes go far beyond the limits of its enquiry and make metaphysical statements about human meaning and destiny.

● The results of science during this century have arguably led to more carnage than all previous religious wars. The consequences of the practice of both science and faith should never be ignored.

● The Christian faith provides scientists with the foundations for ethical research that give value to, and respect for, the world because it is God's creation.

● The claims of the Christian faith are based on evidence that can and should be evaluated by both scientists and non-scientists alike. Faith is about a relationship, and more than measurement.

4. How on earth can a Christian be a scientist?

Psalm 111:2 says, 'Great are the works of the Lord; they are pondered by all who delight in them.' These words are written above the entrance to several university laboratories around the world. They represent a desire to recognise that in doing science, human beings are not attempting to push God from the world (though some might want to do that for personal reasons), but to recognise that they see his handiwork in it.

This is often called natural theology as opposed to a theology of revelation. But it is unhelpful to make too rigid a distinction between them. Often Christians may find it easy to say, 'The Bible is important in telling me everything about life, and Jesus provides the way. I don't need anything else.' None of that is wrong, but it is to misunderstand the totality of biblical witness. God did not merely fashion creation as a backdrop to making mankind. God saw that *all* he had made was very good (Genesis 1:31).

$$E = MC^2$$

God did not merely fashion creation as a backdrop to making mankind. God saw that *all* he had made was very good (Genesis 1:31).

If God is so interested in his creation, why should his followers not be so too? 'For God so loved the world that he gave his one and only Son . . .' (John 3:16). The

32

biblical word for 'world' used in this verse is *kosmos*, and it implies more than simply mankind. If Christians are not interested in God's world around them, they restrict God to their personal life, and imply that he is only interested in their individual destiny. Theologians of the nineteenth century fell into this trap. They were so certain that the world science seemed to uncover was <u>deterministic</u>, a world where God's direct action was excluded, that they were forced to retreat into a mystical world of feelings and personal morality.

If we reject the idea that God gave intelligibility and order to the universe, discovered through the insights of science, the only option left is to scurry back into the world of superstition and make-believe. To do that is to reject the rationality and the wisdom God gave us. The theologian Charles Raven pointed out that the way in which science is done is not science's own patented invention. Observation and interpretation and experiment are common activities. Different standards of verification and different criteria of testing will be applied by different disciplines, of course, but in many respects 'we are all scientists now'. No one should ever ask of someone enquiring about the Christian faith to suspend his or her discriminating faculties.

$$E=MC^2$$

If we reject the idea that God gave intelligibility and order to the universe, discovered through the insights of science, the only option left is to scurry back into the world of superstition and make-believe.

It was the Christian worldview that provided a basis for the method and practice of science. A rational God had created a rational universe, one that could be studied without fear or favour. In Old Testament times, gods of nature were more to be feared and appeased. One did not go poking one's nose into the actions of such minor deities. To do so would invite reprisals.

Unlocking the secrets of God's creation is exciting, and that is why so many young Christians follow a scientific vocation. They may spend months or even years in research where the struggle for a breakthrough never comes. But no scientist ever imagines that there is no such thing as a breakthrough. Because there is rationality to the universe, a solution to a problem does exist. The sense of discovery is deeply satisfying when it does come.

The Christian understands that humanity's discernment and God's are not exactly the same (Isaiah 58:8). Yet until this century much scientific insight followed basic laws of logic and common-sense. Then with the discovery of relativity (see Question 7) and quantum mechanics (see Question 18) something far stranger began to be unravelled. People began to realise that at its roots the universe possessed a deeper logic. Exploration of the fabric of the universe now shows us that it is built on different principles to achieve the structure that appears to us so rationally transparent.

It is this ability of science to knock our paradigms (see Question 1) that should appeal to the Christian. Nothing is ever 'sewn up' in our understanding of the universe. The same is true when we seek knowledge of God. A disciple of Isaac Newton, Pierre Simon, Marquis de Laplace (1749–1827), applied Newton's law of gravity to the solar system. Later he wrote a huge volume suggesting that by knowing all the starting conditions of the universe everything was perfectly predictable. When he related this to Napoleon, it is alleged that Napoleon enquired where this left God. Laplace is said to have replied, 'Sir, I have no need of that hypothesis.' Science has grown up since then in professing a humility towards what it knows about the cosmos (see Question 26).

A Christian scientist, then, should not be tempted to put faith into a compartment insulated from the discoveries of science. Science provides a limited but discerning rationality in its description of the universe, but by no means excludes its originator.

$$E = MC^2$$

Science provides a limited but discerning rationality in its description of the universe, but by no means excludes its originator.

This is not to imply that there will be no problems in reintegrating the worlds of science and faith. The phenomena of providence and the miraculous which refer to God working in his world still demand explanations (see Question 37), but such events are not excluded because the clockwork and certain world of Laplace no longer holds sway. Because of this, Christians can be scientists with the same assurance which was held in the early days of science when discovery was seen as using our God-given intelligence to explore his universe. We can still realise what glory it reveals of the creator (Psalm 19:1).

Sum-up

● A rational creator has led to a rational universe that can be understood.

● A Christian who is a scientist is seeking to understand God's handiwork.

● If we deny the God-given intelligibility and order of the universe, the only option left is to scurry back into the world of magic and make-believe.

● Twentieth-century science has discovered that our world is less closed to God's presence. A Christian can be a scientist with integrity.

5. With Galileo's discoveries the church got it wrong and he got it right. Wasn't this the start of science showing the errors of religious belief?

Two major battles have been fought historically between science and religion. These are the controversy with Galileo about the motion of the earth in the early seventeenth century, and the Darwinian debate on evolution in the mid-nineteenth century (see Question 23). In both of them the public perception is that decisive blows were dealt to the church, and faith retreated into areas science had not explored. People assume faith has been retreating ever since.

These controversies cannot be reduced to impersonal debate. They are both better understood in light of the personalities and the circumstances of the time, and of later partisan interpretation. The church was largely concerned with saving souls in its early history, and engaging in philosophical speculation was hardly on its agenda. Hence in their enthusiasm to speak to their contemporaries Christians used current ideas from popular thought.

$$E = MC^2$$

The church was largely concerned with saving souls in its early history, and engaging in philosophical speculation was hardly on its agenda.

When it came to theories about the universe, the model of Greek philosopher Claudius Ptolemy lasted for over 1,400 years. A modification of Aristotle's view of the universe, it held that the earth was at the centre of the universe and the planets and the sun moved around it. The planets were perfect spheres and their orbits were circles in an unchanging heaven. The Greeks liked circles, and since the earth feels stationary it was considered to be at the centre of the universe long before Ptolemy.

Ptolemy noticed that this model needed modification. When the motion of the planets was followed it was observed that they would appear to reverse direction for a while and then turn back to their original direction. To explain this the simple circular orbits had to have smaller circular orbits (called epicycles) added to them. Other corrections were needed to get better agreement with observation, but the implications were not greatly worried about.

The church accepted Ptolemy's ideas, for they were hardly at loggerheads with a God who cared for his world. Other thinkers had put the sun at the centre, yet it was not until 1543 that Ptolemy was seriously questioned. Nicholas Copernicus, a Polish priest, published a theory that put the sun at the centre of the known universe, with planets in circular orbits around it. Although this new theory also agreed with observations of planetary motion, it was not exact and wasn't really a great improvement on the Ptolemaic system.

$$E = MC^2$$

The church accepted Ptolemy's ideas, for they were hardly at loggerheads with a God who cared for his world.

At this time the Protestant Reformation was consolidating itself and dealing with the inevitable backlash from the Roman Catholic Church. New freedoms promoted the study of astronomy and experimentation in

Protestant northern Europe. Yet the father of experimentation is popularly taken to be Galileo Galilei, who was a Roman Catholic. Galileo was a successful entrepreneur, and a mathematics professor in Venice, which was then the chief cosmopolitan city of the Mediterranean world. In 1609 he perfected a telescope which could magnify ten times. With it he observed moons revolving around Jupiter, and saw in great detail the craters on our moon. Both observations contradicted the Ptolemaic model where the planets were perfect spheres and all circled the earth. He also saw the phases of Venus, which implied that Venus moved around the sun.

In 1609 Johannes Kepler, a German Lutheran, published his findings that the planets moved in elliptical orbits. He calculated the distance of the planets from the sun and the time they took to revolve around it. Ptolemy's complicated theory of epicycles was redundant and Kepler saw this new simplicity as evidence of God's design. Galileo, though, who seems not to have acknowledged Kepler, had a rather worse time in Catholic Italy. Galileo published his book *Starry Messenger* in 1610, which related his observations and highlighted the errors of Ptolemy.

The Counter-Reformation had been gaining pace for most of the previous half century and with the Thirty Years War about to begin (in 1618) the political situation was tense, and Galileo could not afford to be indiscreet. In 1616 he got permission from a leading cardinal that would allow him to discuss Copernicus' theory as a hypothesis but not teach it as established fact. In 1623 a new pope was elected and Galileo went to speak to him. Although the Roman Church had taken on board the earlier ideas of astronomer Tycho Brahé (who held that the sun went round the earth, and other planets went round the sun), nevertheless it was reluctant to adopt this in troubled times.

In 1632, following the publication of a new book *Dialogue on the Great World Systems*, Galileo gave the Copernican theory too much praise and little criticism. The characters he sketched arguing against Copernican theory he portrayed as 'less able'! This was unwise and he was reported, and the book was withdrawn. After a show trial and under threat of torture he recanted. He lived under house arrest, now being over seventy years old. He continued his experiments in mechanics; the conditions were cordial, and he was allowed visitors. Subsequently, scientists found it hard to get sponsors in the Catholic world, but that did not stop them working entirely.

The politics then outweighed both the theology and the science. It was not a simple case of the church shutting its eyes to science. The Reformers were happy to allow the new discoveries of experimental science, for their constitution led them to cling less to church tradition and dogma. Paradigms were harder to shift in the Catholic world, however.

$$E = MC^2$$

The Reformers were happy to allow the new discoveries of experimental science, for their constitution led them to cling less to church tradition and dogma.

Some Christians have believed that the issue of biblical inerrancy is at stake in this argument. Psalm 104:3 and 1 Chronicles 16:30 are often cited as verses that seem to support the older view of the universe. Both are verses within hymns of praise to the God of order. St Augustine had recognised long before that the Bible was not attempting to instruct people about things other than those of relevance to their salvation, or to be 'concerned with the form and shape of the heavens'. It was not meant to be the prime scientific text. Undoubtedly the Roman Catholic Church wished to discover the truth, or else it would not have allowed Galileo to debate the point for twenty-two years. One Carmelite monk actually wrote a book in 1616 saying that the Copernican system was consistent with the Bible! A leading Jesuit, Christopher Clavius, also recognised that the old (non-Christian) model of the universe needed changing.

$$E = MC^2$$

Undoubtedly the Roman Catholic Church wished to discover the truth, or else it would not have allowed Galileo to debate the point for twenty-two years.

Galileo did indeed get it right; but his failure was in diplomacy and in the lack of better evidence. Galileo offended his patrons and sponsors – a fatal mistake even for scientists today. However, it should also be noticed that Galileo did not have a watertight case, because if the earth did move, then the stars should also appear to move as the earth rotates around the sun. Until 1838 this 'parallax' effect was too small to be observed, as telescopes were too feeble.

If science needs to learn a lesson about the need to communicate diplomatically, then the church must also beware taking on unrefined scientific notions too hastily. The church was right in being cautious initially, but injudicious in hanging on to Ptolemy's ideas.[2]

Science and religion often tend to be prescriptive before new theories are fully developed. It was Francis

Bacon who in his book *New Method* (1620) warned that we should all beware grasping at new insights. Both Galileo and his inquisitors were found wanting, and the truth suffered as a result. This controversy may seem to suggest that science and religion are always going to be opponents battling for supremacy, but this need not be so (see Question 7). Science can flourish in a seedbed of inquisitive faith, and faith can flourish when it recognises the faithfulness of a loving God whose works are seen in human discovery. Neither side needed to bull-doze the other in the Galileo controversy. Strong personalities and vested interests fuelled this argument. It has lasted in the public mind to the detriment of the Christian faith.

Science and religion often tend to be prescriptive
before new theories are fully developed.

Sum-up

- The Galileo affair was not a simple matter of the church instantly condemning what it thought challenged faith. Both scientists and Christians were seeking truth.

- The affair was a problem for the Catholic church coping with the uncertain times of the Counter-Reformation, yet Galileo was allowed to advance his ideas for over twenty years.

- Although Galileo's condemnation was an error, his ideas and those of Kepler continued and were seen as uncovering the mysteries of God's universe.

6. Isn't it true that science makes progress that is obvious, and it betters our lives, while religions seem to make nothing but trouble and never get anywhere?

It is undeniable that without science we would still be living in something resembling medieval times. Monks would treat illnesses; writing would be with quill pens; no books would be freely available, and the benefits of computers would not be felt. There would be no rapid transport to work, or to well-equipped hospitals in emergencies. As a result, it is claimed that science has done much to improve the world, whereas religions never seem to get anywhere.

But this scientific technological revolution has come at a price. Science makes the world the object of its study and consequently readily sees the world's resources at the mercy of its resultant technologies. Stop scientific progress around the mid-nineteenth century and we could strike off a number of items that have recently become our lot. We would have weapons that were less effective at mass killing, minimal chemical pollution, and no pressing threat from nuclear waste or noxious car exhausts. Dispel the idea that science never causes trouble; twentieth-century history cannot let the scientist off as an innocent bystander or someone just following orders.

$$E = MC^2$$

Dispel the idea that science never causes trouble; twentieth-century history cannot let the scientist off as an innocent bystander.

Despite these technological headaches, though, science is a rigorous attempt to create an understanding of the world, and understanding is preferable to ignorance. Repeatable experiments help build mathematical models that attempt to comprehend what is going on in a complex world. Precisely because the world is so complex, science is a subject that builds upon previous knowledge and inevitably makes progress in understanding.

Good theories will always suggest more than experiments can find out, and it is this that spurs scientists on. As science delves deeper and deeper into the minutiae of the rational world, the sheer intricacy and abundance of detail is almost overwhelming. The Greeks thought that as you divided matter you got to an indivisible limit, which they called the atom. They were wrong. Scientific investigation will never end, for as the structures of the world are examined ever more deeply, there is always more to discover. Progress is needed because solutions to harder and harder problems are now being sought, such as possible cures for cancer.

By contrast, what do religions do? They are certainly a powerful source of inspiration for art and literature and the spur for ethics. The hospitals that are technologically equipped today originated from religious belief in a caring God committed to his world, and one who was interested in its sustenance (Deuteronomy 11:12) and its redemption (John 3:16). Hospitals are a reflection of the healing love of Jesus Christ shown in his earthly ministry. When people realise that God is interested in his world they are encouraged to be interested in it too. Without that example, why bother about the poor or the sick? It is in this manner that a religion such as Christianity has made progress in the world.

$$E = MC^2$$

When people realise that God is interested in his
world they are encouraged to be interested in it too.

The world of science is that of restricted and controlled experimentation, but that of religion is intimately
involved with the uncontrolled human condition outside the laboratory. Religious folk live in the real world,
and conflict does arise from the existence of many different religions. It is this diversity that prompts the suspicion that religions never get anywhere. Why are there
so many, and why do they disagree, unlike science?

You could suggest that with many differing cultures
across the world there are bound to be different religions. All are inculturated to some extent because they
all start in some specific place and their initial communication is in terms that local people understand. Yet
they not only relate to local matters; they also make
statements about ultimate reality. This is because cultural questions can only usually be answered by stepping
outside the culture. So a body of conceptual knowledge
is built up that provides answers to why things exist or
happen that go beyond questions about what is tangible
or repeatable.

Religions then quickly move to the big questions of
life, such as: Does God exist? If he does, what has he
said to us? If he loves us, why do we suffer (see
Question 36)? Is suffering real or an illusion? Theologian
John Bowker has pointed out that religions are so dangerous precisely because they *do* ask ultimate questions,
and these questions are of supreme, life-changing
importance. Religious conflict arises because of these
high stakes.

Scientists rarely tackle the ultimate and more person-ally challenging questions. This detachment from life and history has led to a lack of ethical awareness (see Question 3) and the popular view of science as chilling-ly impersonal. The speed of progress has led also to a denial of the importance of history. Scientific papers over thirty years old rarely have a direct relevance to frontline research. Science becomes uncoupled from the wisdom of its past and the motivations for it. It can then become prey to commercial forces that have agendas which differ from those of the past (see Questions 15 and 47). Although religions are seen by some people to be stuck in the past, tradition often provides an existing means to evaluate future action. So often in science, as in the cases of Thalidomide[3] and BSE, society is left to clear up after it.

If both religion and science make progress that can be seen in retrospect as both good and bad, then is there a common way forward? Perhaps one answer is found in the notion of falsifiability in science (see Question 2). Religions also have internal consistency and cogency (as far as their mystery allows) or else they would have few followers, but objective falsifiability is difficult (try proving that God doesn't exist or miracles don't happen if you're unsure about this). Both scientists and religious adherents commit themselves to their own beliefs in order to promote them. Yet both need humility in doing so. Mutual respect in these different disciplines is part of the key to their public acceptability. The message may be that one's own religion or scientific knowledge gives access to ultimate meaning, but it should be pursued within a framework which recognis-es that others can stumble upon some important truths too (1 Peter 3:15).

$$E = MC^2$$

Both scientists and religious adherents commit themselves to their own beliefs in order to promote them. Yet both need humility in doing so.

In his ministry Jesus always gave his followers the freedom to leave (John 6:66). But to those who realised that in him was a pearl of great price (Matthew 13:45–46), the promise of eternal life was given. This element of the Christian faith provides the impetus for hope and an implicit responsibility for the future (see Question 42). Both science and religion make progress and promote understanding and controlled progress when they recognise the great responsibilities arising from the outcomes that they advance.

Sum-up

● Science works, but it often does so with little recognition of the consequences. It has led to many advances that have been far from beneficial.

● Religions are dangerous because they ask ultimate questions and challenge people personally. But answers to these questions can provide direction for human behaviour that is beneficial.

● Science and religion as bodies of understanding do make progress, but they must each recognise the responsibilities that ensue from this.

7. Once we know the mechanism for how things work we have a complete picture of them. Surely religious questions that ask 'why' and refer to purpose have no validity?

Every day in my household there is a ritual when the postman comes. My three Springer spaniels keep listening for the sound of the post office van turning into the drive. They can observe the postman driving up to the front door (we live in a rural area where such things still happen), and they bark repeatedly until, after delivering the post, he has retreated with a friendly wave. The dogs could describe (if they were able to communicate with me verbally) the mechanism of the event, but they would not have the slightest idea as to the purpose of letters. They could outline the exact mechanistic truth of the visit but have no clue as to its meaning, or the reason for the postman's existence.

Around 325 BC the Greek philosopher Aristotle suggested that explanations could be broken down into four 'causes', or ways in which answers to questions could be put. The material cause described what a thing was made of, and the efficient cause described that which initiated the happening. These answer the 'how' questions. The formal cause explained things in terms of form or properties, and the final cause gave the reason or the goal for the event. These latter causes related more to the question of 'why'. Science cannot properly answer 'why' questions except to say, 'It just is.' Why does anything exist? It just does. Why is the universe so rationally transparent to beings in one small part of it? It just is. Going beyond this is to step into

48

purpose and meaning and into <u>metaphysics</u>.

$$E = MC^2$$

Science cannot properly answer 'why' questions
except to say, 'It just is.'

Half a century after Galileo and Kepler championed experimentation (see Question 5), Sir Isaac Newton discovered the law of gravity that governed the motion of the planets. By assuming the same law applied everywhere, on earth and in the heavens, he was able to explain details of the orbit of the planets in the known universe. To observers it seemed like clockwork, both predictable and certain.

Newton never discovered the cause of gravity, yet its simplicity, in mathematical terms, was profound. From his laws it was calculated that the solar system was probably stable. But this simplicity led people to presume that all nature was transparently obvious, which twentieth-century science has begun to discover is not the case.

Before Newton's theories, the courses of the planets had been ascribed to the direct working of God and the stability of the solar system to his faithfulness. He alone ordered the heavens and their motions. But now a simple law apparently 'explained' it all. With no explanations of why things behaved as they did, God's will seemed to suffice as explanation of both motive and mechanism. Once scientific mechanisms were proposed, it appeared that the existence of God's will was called into question. Motive was eclipsed, and mechanism became muddled with metaphysics.

$$E = MC^2$$

Once scientific mechanisms were proposed, it
appeared that the existence of God's will was called
into question.

In the early days of science not much was understood,
from the causes of illnesses to the weather. So it was rel-
atively easy to leave God as the direct 'explanation' of
many happenings. The providence of God provided the
process. Yet as science progressed, the area left to God
began to contract. He became the 'God of the gaps' and
explanations of events in terms of 'acts of God' became
less acceptable as the gaps shrank. Some Christians still
relate to this god today. So one reads things like, 'The
bee needs God to fly.' But such a statement is not really
an example of faith. God then becomes the plug to close
the gap of inadequacy in our physical understanding.
Frequently, solutions are found (as has been true in the
case of the bee) and God apparently becomes pushed
further off stage.

Some scientists alas have deliberately continued this
category confusion of metaphysics and mechanics. Since
science makes progress (see Question 6), God seems certain to lose in such a rigged game. Some even go so far
as to assert that knowing the mechanism of any event is
sufficient to provide the complete explanation of it.
Answering the 'how' question provides the sum total of
all there is to know.

Such a claim is not new in history, however. In the
thirteenth century Thomas Aquinas argued with
philosophers who had rediscovered Aristotle's works.
Their claim for the autonomy of 'scientific' knowledge
challenged theology. Aquinas maintained that science

(meaning a body of knowledge derived from the senses) and religion could together provide a complementary understanding of the world. 'Some truths may be obtained through the experience of the senses, and others can be gained through revelation. God, said Aquinas, is beyond <u>empirical</u> observation, though not beyond inference or relationship. All these truths can be mediated through one's intellect, so reason and revelation can both be valid ways of acquiring knowledge.

$$E = MC^2$$

Reason and revelation can both be valid ways of acquiring knowledge.

Difficult questions are likely to fall upon those who claim that only 'how' questions have meaning. They have to consider the existence of love, or the appreciation of music, or religious awareness. Such a narrow view is itself a rival metaphysical suggestion to theism. Proponents of radical Darwinism attempt to promote this view in disciplines like sociobiology in which human values like altruism are 'explained' in terms of animal behaviour (see Question 28). The results look like lame, one-dimensional pictures when compared with the richness of the real world. Just because meaning and value are excluded from scientific investigation doesn't mean they don't exist. In fact scientific enterprise requires people to perform with all their genius, creativity, judgement and experience to gain insight.

Science, then, is unable to provide answers to all the questions that arise from the insights that it gives. Its approach limits what it can say. Yet it offers to religion knowledge of how the world works and therefore provides a commentary on the Book of Nature written by

God. But religion has to embrace all forms of human insight because the God to whom it refers is the Author of everything. It is the supplier of answers to meta-questions – questions that go beyond and ask often simply, 'Why do things exist as they do at all?'

To ask only 'why' questions is to be ignorant of the marvellous intricacy of the world God has made, sustains and cares for (Hebrews 1:3). To ask only 'how' questions is to starve human beings of the richness of perception that God himself has given to us (Psalm 8:4). Because we recognise this, 'why' questions will continue to fascinate us. Science may explain mechanisms and remove mystery, but it cannot dispel awe and wonder.

Sum-up

- As God is creator and sustainer, the absence of any mechanistic explanation for events often defaulted to direct divine agency.

- Early discoveries such as those by Newton provided deceptively simple and apparently complete solutions to observations in nature.

- Metaphysics became muddled with mechanism as scientific knowledge asserted itself as the only form of true knowledge.

- Religion must be consonant with the world of experience, but it asks questions that go beyond empirical observations. They are real questions that are worth answering.

8. Mathematics explains everything. Surely we don't need God at all!

Mathematics is the tool by which science explores the remarkable rationality in the world. Like it or loathe it, it is indispensable. And it is indispensable because as physicist Eugene Wigner once commented, there is a glaring presupposition as we study the universe of 'the unreasonable effectiveness of mathematics'. Mathematics works. Astronomer Sir James Jeans once said that 'God is a mathematician'. From the time of Archimedes and his simple mechanics, and ancient astronomers who predicted eclipses, mathematics has been gainfully employed in explaining how things work. Physical theories that fit experimental facts are expressed time after time in a mathematical beauty that evokes wonder.

$$E = MC^2$$

Physical theories that fit experimental facts are expressed time after time in a mathematical beauty that evokes wonder.

We might be further amazed when we realise that we can do mathematics at all. Although some people find it difficult, it can be understood (with a patient enough teacher!). It is surprising that we can understand the mathematical structure of our universe. Sir Roger Penrose, Professor of Mathematics at Oxford, recognised that although some of this ability may be the product of evolution (see Question 23), it is hard to see how a selective pressure to do mathematics would be advantageous when compared with more utilitarian pursuits like hunting. Additionally, we are able to think abstractly. Some mathematics cannot be put into pictorial form, such as that of quantum mechanics (see Questions 17 and 18). It is hard to see what benefit such abstract abilities could give us, unless somehow we are thinking the creator's thoughts long after he did (Psalm 139:17).

Some scientists have been carried away by the beauty and perspicacity of mathematics. Theoretical chemist Peter Atkins boldly states that 'physical reality is mathematics and mathematics is physical reality'.[4] Material reality and mathematical reality, he suggests, share the same logical structures – perhaps they are the same thing!

One of the snares which those who do mathematics can fall into is what philosopher A. N. Whitehead called 'misplaced concreteness', of seeing mathematics as the reality instead of being a description of reality. When applied to reality, mathematics describes the relationships between things – it is not necessarily the same as being those things. Abstract mathematics need not relate to reality at all.

$$E = MC^2$$

Abstract mathematics need not relate to
reality at all.

By way of example, consider the force of gravity. Newton's law gave a mathematical description of it. However, the law said nothing about what gravity actually was. Later, Albert Einstein, in his <u>General Theory of</u>

Relativity, provided further insight when he recognised that gravity could also be represented mathematically as being caused by the curving of space (more properly, space and time considered together). However, even with such insight, we might legitimately ask, 'What exactly is curved spacetime?'[5]

In addition, mathematics can provide further insight. It is also possible to describe gravity as being due to the exchange of theoretical particles called gravitons. These are effectively different mathematical ways of describing the same effect. But they are not themselves the effect. So although mathematics is the most necessary and powerful tool of a scientist, it only provides limited insight into solving problems. It cannot supply meta-physical answers to questions about the nature of reality.

In 1931 Kurt Gödel proved that any consistent mathematical theory containing the arithmetic use of numbers like 0, 1, 2, 3, etc. will always contain statements which can't be proved or disproved from itself alone. It must always contain things called axioms, which are propositions that must be taken on trust to further knowledge. Such 'gaps' in our understanding are probably an irreducible part of our universe. Using them to reinforce belief in a creator God is not therefore to smuggle in a 'god of the gaps' (see Question 7).

Mathematics has been effective in providing a way of describing what we see around us. But its descriptive power is often only approximate and its models imperfect. At present we cannot tell whether mathematics is prescriptive (that is, it exists beyond us) or descriptive (a function of our minds fathoming the universe). Our laws of the natural sciences may indeed be the laws of nature. At present it is only possible to say that they very nearly are. We will probably never gain a complete insight into understanding reality, despite the power of mathematics (see also Question 19).

$$E = MC^2$$

We will probably never gain a complete insight into understanding reality, despite the power of mathematics.

Finally, Roger Penrose has suggested that the best mathematical insights just come in a flash, as a kind of revelation from above. This may be true, and certainly our insights into questions about ultimate reality and meaning seem to come more from revelation than reason. For a Christian this consonance is something that is more likely to be true if there is a God who is a mathematician.

Sum-up

- Physical theories that fit experimental facts are expressed in a mathematical beauty that is amazing. The effectiveness of mathematics is axiomatic and must be taken on trust.

- Some scientists consider that mathematical theories are actually as real as material reality itself.

- Christians would want to acknowledge that the mathematics of creation is neither solely descriptive nor prescriptive but rather reflects the wisdom of its creator.

9. The Christian faith was based on an old idea that heaven was in the clouds somewhere. We now know that's not true, so why not ditch Christianity?

Science is a fast-changing discipline. School and university textbooks are never in print for very long before the tide of discovery uncovers new insights that sweep away old models and structures. The lecturer's confidential-type statement 'You were told this at one stage [GCSE, A-level, etc.], but now I'll explain it properly' is the result of a relentless search for better explanations of events. However, we still need a simple basis for science. A ten-year-old is not taught science beginning with quantum theory, for example (see Question 17). A wise teacher accommodates her message so that her pupils will understand it, and also that she may stretch their imaginations. Eventually she may teach complex theories. What is important is that the insights that the pupils gain on the way are often invaluable in later comprehension of such complexities.

A wise teacher accommodates her message so that her pupils will understand it.

In a similar way, theologian John Calvin noted that God communicated in an accommodating way so that all people might understand his message. In fact, the more we understand the cultural background of the Bible, the greater is our understanding of the truths of the gospel message. Early Christians communicated the

existence of a God who cared for his creation by using
the thought forms of their day. Each generation does
this in order to be effective communicators. To ignore
this cultural divide, or to assume that biblical writings
can be read off directly without cultural discernment, is
to treat biblical truths like oracles or mathematical
axioms. For example, the value of Jesus' parable of the
prodigal son is timeless, but becomes all the more hard-
hitting when one realises that elderly fathers of the day
never ran (Luke 15:20)!

Because both science and faith have their reference
points in the world around us, there will be times when
scientific knowledge of the world moves our faith on.
The God we know is neither beyond the sky, nor even
'out there' in space, as a Soviet cosmonaut once
quipped. Our faith matures and deepens when it is better informed about God's creation.

However, this doesn't mean we have altogether
explained away the objection in the question. Consider
the events of the ascension. What worries people *is* the
point that there *is* this cultural gap in understanding.
The disciples appear sure their Lord had begun a great
return to the heavens 'up there', and that there was a
throne room where he sat down at the right hand of
God (Mark 16:19). We might forgive them, for how else
could they picture it or proclaim it in the thought forms
of the day? If some movement were necessary to por-
tray 'going away', then it was better up than down! That
was surely the purpose behind what actually happened.
It was a kind of acted parable by the Lord, which
accommodated itself to them.

This is not to deny that the biblical witnesses had any
genuine spiritual insight, nor imply that they made it all
up. In fact it is the lack of mythological embellishment

in the account that suggests the event happened rather than being a later projection of the belief that Jesus went to heaven. The accounts are so matter of fact that we might almost wish there were more. And yet from the ascension the disciples recognised that in the ascended Jesus there was a new quality of life that was already available. The potency of the simple concept of a heaven above is what made the ascension an event understandable for all generations to come, even if we now picture these realities in a more sophisticated way.

$$E = MC^2$$

The potency of the simple concept of a heaven above is what made the ascension an event understandable for all generations to come.

How then can we understand such events in the light of our own ideas about space and time? Can verses such as 2 Kings 1:12, Psalm 14:2 and John 6:33 *only* be read as portraying a literal heaven 'up there beyond the clouds'? Can we gain insight from them any more, as scientists do from their simplified models?

Unfortunately, we are as much intellectual children of dualist Descartes as we are spiritual children of monotheistic Abraham. Consequently, we still tend to think of the material and the spiritual realms as utterly separate. In some ways we are worse off than in Bible times, where the awe and mystery of the world was far more integrated into everyday life. Yet we must picture divine events as much in terms of our own worldviews as they needed to in theirs. We all need frames of reference. It is just that ours are much harder to find in a largely spiritually barren and materialistic culture.

In the past few years some theologians have been dismissive of these older frameworks that have been so useful. The label 'mythical' has been given to many biblical events, which has popularly been understood as meaning 'untrue'. This is to miss the point that a framework is needed to understand such events. In practice, it is usually events that precede insights, rather than the other way round. C. S. Lewis, an expert in legends and mythology, once remarked that the events of the life of Jesus do not look like cleverly devised myths (2 Peter 1:16). The Bible accounts look rather like reportage, even though some of it was clearly not understood at the time, yet was necessarily reported in the thought forms of the day.

Growing up in knowledge may mean we can no longer play with the toy models of old ideas, yet this is our loss. But the startling biblical insight which their crude cosmology *could* picture, was that the final destiny for humankind would not be a victory for either a heaven of incorporeal forms or an earthly hell of material decay. Rather the event of the resurrection of Jesus (see Question 41) showed them a new reality in which both were united appropriately in new dimensions of time and space replacing the old ones. Perhaps the disciples' insights were not as invalid as the models they were compelled to use. One day we may understand better the necessary integration of the spiritual and material elements of our makeup, and build upon the wisdom of the past (see also Questions 28, 31 and 34).

$$E = MC^2$$

The disciples' insights were not as invalid as the models they were compelled to use.

Sum-up

- Those who wrote of and preached about Jesus needed to do so in a way that would be understandable then. This is equally true today.

- Old views of the universe were the means by which the experiences of the day could be understood. Today we must use new frames of reference that have grown from the old, recognising though that the old will still contain valuable insights.

- Today our new scientific theories of the universe may enable us to reinvest in the gospel of resurrection and ascension where the 'material' is not denigrated in terms of the 'spiritual'.

10. Science has continued largely unchecked this century. What, if anything, can Christianity contribute to stem the worries about its effects in the coming years?

Many people are as suspicious of science today as they are of religion. In its thirst for knowledge and desire for experimentation, science appears to be unrestrained in its execution. Despite the undoubted benefits, the popular fear is that if it *can* be done, then sooner or later it will be. Will science spearhead the construction of a nightmare brave new world? Many fear it will. Also today, people are just as likely to question the validity of truths expressed in scientific findings as those of religion. In science, the commercialism that drives research is recognised more fully, and often considered as suspect. In the last decades when scientific research has produced results that conveniently assisted sponsoring companies, it is not surprising that respect for science has fallen. Science is not thought to be impartial any more.

$$E = MC^2$$

The popular fear about science is that if it *can* be done, then sooner or later it will be.

The reason for this fear is also due to the phenomenal growth of science (see Question 6). Up until the 1950s it was just about possible for any scientist to have a reasonable comprehension of the wide variety of research going on in the world. There were a few able scientists who would read most of the scientific papers produced each year. Today the output is so vast that it is not only impossible to read them, but impossible even to read the one-paragraph summaries of papers (called abstracts). Consequently, the community of scientists is fragmented. For example, a nuclear scientist may understand the safety issues concerning a nuclear power plant, but not the ecological impact of its waste products.

This inevitable specialisation has led scientists to fail to address the issue of responsibility. This is not to imply that scientists are irresponsible, but to recognise that the fragmentary nature of science has led to a dilution of practical considerations of who, if anyone, is accountable not only to humanity, but to the world itself. The BSE crisis partly arose from an unknowingly crucial decision to reduce the temperature for preparing cattle feed (a subject for food technologists), without recognising that certain brain chemicals called prion proteins would consequently not be broken down, and would be allowed through, intact, into the food chain (an issue for environmental biology and human physiology).[6]

In the past there was also an expectation that unsolved problems of technology would be addressed in some rosy scientific future when knowledge had advanced sufficiently. For example, the cheap electricity of nuclear power was promoted on a hope of future generations taking responsibility for nuclear waste and dealing with it. Some account was taken at the time, but we are now recognising that the ecological, social and environmental impacts are far greater than a more culturally remote and unchecked scientific community imagined in the past.

Unfettered science, with unlimited budgets, is a thing of the past. Pure research (research for the sake of it, with no immediate spin-offs) is getting harder and harder to sustain, for in a world of tightening budgets, returns are more keenly sought, and profits are likely to dictate direction. Scientific research that provides rapid commercial returns is more likely to survive. With this pressure, the need for caution through regulation becomes ever more acute, and it is required by an increasingly wary public. The advent of the genetic modification of organisms such as plants for food highlights this. It is not just a matter of education or a reassertion of scientific authority, but a recognition that there may be limits which society feels as an instinctive response it is wrong to transgress (see Question 42). But this requires a value system involving an assessment of the limits of exploitation, and a worldwide approach and framework for ethical response.

$$E=MC^2$$

Unfettered science, with unlimited budgets, is a thing of the past.

A new challenge to religion is generated as science comes out of the laboratory and impacts on the world as never before. Increasingly, the world looks to other institutions to challenge science's power and direction. If the church wishes to have a voice today, it cannot neglect to contribute to the debate on how to take on this inevitable corporate responsibility. Those who live in a scientifically oriented world will find it odd if a religion is world-denying, yet still says it has something to contribute to lifestyle choices today. In 1996 theologian/scientist Ronald Cole-Turner voiced concern that the church often acted as if the kingdom of God and our world were mutually exclusive places. Yet if God and spirituality and moral obligation have any place at all, they must have a place and meaning in this one world, which God has created – the world explored by science and technology. God set Adam in Eden to be a gardener, yet we are much more adept at being exploiters and looters. It is *this* world that God will renew, and we are accountable for it (Psalm 104:30; Revelation 21:2–3).

The incarnation of Jesus Christ will always form a major part of the basis for a Christian response. God has made but one physical world, and it is this world that Christ came to redeem, not to discard (Romans 8:22–23). He came to redeem us from wickedness, not from our surroundings (Titus 2:14), and to inaugurate the kingdom of God. This was his priority message (Mark 1:15). It included the relief of suffering and evil influence (Mark 1:34), cruelty (Mark 1:44), forgiveness (Mark 2:5) and the pursuit of righteousness and justice especially for the poor, the oppressed and the marginalised (Luke 4:18–19). Jesus challenges us about our motives, and to follow him in a life lived for others.

'What would Jesus do?' might seem to be a simplistic slogan,[7] but without some reference point, our current economic powers will continue to set the rules and happily control science. Where better to begin the questioning of scientific commercialisation than with the one who warned us about the danger of serving 'mammon' (Matthew 6:24, RSV), the god of money?

$$E=MC^2$$

Where better to begin the questioning of scientific commercialisation than with the one who warned us about the danger of serving 'mammon'?

As redeemed people of God, Christians need not

think their input should be solely negative. If we follow the Christ who healed the sick, then medical advances that relieve certain illnesses will surely be acceptable (see also Question 43). Of course, there will be many grey areas and ethical disagreements, but boundaries, even if arbitrary or provisional, will help to give to science the necessary limits it needs to have today. The challenge to religions worldwide is to engage in such debate over policy-making. We are getting ever better at messing up our world and the challenge is daily more pressing.

Sum-up

- Science is as much feared today as admired because of its unimpeded escalation and commercial involvement.

- This has led to the urgent need for ethical regulation that recognises the interrelated functioning of all creation, including that of humanity with its environment.

- Christians need to engage in this debate, recognising the call of Jesus to proclaim the implications of this being God's creation, and of its need for redemption.

LITTLE AND LARGE
Cosmology and the quantum world

11. If I believe the Big Bang happened, then where does God fit in? Hasn't modern science disproved the Bible?

Why should we believe in the Big Bang? It might seem on the face of it that it is a contender for the divine title – in the beginning was the Big Bang! Many Christians are suspicious of it for precisely that reason. Yet if Christians are honest, they should be as interested to examine the evidence for it as they are to hope others will examine the evidence for the resurrection of Christ (see Question 41).

Christians should be as interested to examine the evidence for the Big Bang as they are to hope others will examine the evidence for the resurrection of Christ.

Until recently the universe was considered to be static and unchanging. But one of the questions asked of Isaac Newton was why everything in the universe didn't get sucked into a single big 'crunch', as his force of gravitation pulled everything together. What was balancing out the whole thing? In 1917 Albert Einstein faced this same problem when producing his model of the universe. He suggested that to keep everything static one needed a force of repulsion, and he added it via a 'cosmological constant' into his equations, an action which he later called 'the biggest mistake of my life'.

In fact it was a Belgian priest, Georges Lemaître, who

suggested that this repulsion had happened initially in the life of the universe by an explosion of what was termed 'the cosmic egg'. When Einstein linked space and time together in his <u>General Theory of Relativity</u>, he suggested that the universe might be expanding and had indicated that this explosion of matter was not into some *pre-existing* space and time, but as matter expanded outwards so space and time did too. St Augustine, in his *Confessions* of AD 397/8, had already suggested that God created time with space, and no time existed before creation. In 1948 George Gamow modified the cosmic egg idea and devised a theory for the start of the universe that became known as 'the Big Bang'. In the first minutes of existence, as the baby universe exploded and simultaneously began to cool, simple chemical elements were formed from their constituent parts that led to all we see today.

Two major pieces of evidence suggested that Gamow and Lemaître were on the right track. In 1929 Edwin Hubble compared the estimated distances to observed galaxies by analysing the light their stars emitted. This light had been found to differ in its frequency signature according to how fast the stars moved away. For almost all galaxies that were not near our own, he found that the more distant the galaxy the faster it was receding. Only local galaxies appear to be slowly coming together under the force of gravity. This suggested that the model of expanding space and matter was correct. We are not at the centre of the universe, but everything in it is moving away from an initial event.

If a Big Bang did occur, then one might expect some residual traces of it to be visible, rather like the warm embers of an old fire. In 1965 Arno Penzias and Robert Wilson stumbled across just this in the form of microwave radiation pervading the whole of the sky. Over the lifetime of the universe this background glow had cooled to just a few degrees above absolute zero (-273°C). Only the Big Bang could readily account for its presence.

From the known rates of expansion we can estimate that the universe is approximately 13–15 <u>billion</u> years old. The newest space telescopes have enabled us to see the most distant galaxies. Light from these has taken around 13 billion years to get here, which gives us a lower limit to the age.

In 1951 Pope Pius XII alluded to the Big Bang in his address to the Pontifical Academy of Sciences. Although he suggested that we should beware of uncritically adopting scientific models of observation into Christian belief (see Question 5), the idea of a creation point, of a temporal beginning, could be readily read from the text of Genesis 1.

However, Genesis 1 is not concerned primarily with giving a detailed account of the beginning. The concern of Bible history is to see how God continually *works* in his creation. He is a God who is true to his nature, keeping his promises, sustaining his world (Psalm 104:29–30; Colossians 1:17; Hebrews 1:3). In fact, medieval churchmen such as Thomas Aquinas realised that it didn't make too much difference if a start point of space and time couldn't be discovered, for biblical history itself records God's continuing care in creation.

Professor Stephen Hawking's quote on creation is well known: '[But] if the universe is really self-contained, having no boundary or edge, it would have neither beginning nor end: it would simply be.' By the words 'self-contained', Hawking meant that at the earliest times the universe is known to have been very small.

Very small things are governed in our world by the laws of quantum theory (see Questions 16 to 18), where time, position and other measurable quantities become indistinct when compared to our macro-world. Hawking applied quantum theory to the early universe. Perhaps no distinct point of creation could be recognised in time, so Hawking goes on, 'What place, then, for a creator?'[8]

The Christian reply is found within the pages of the Bible after Genesis 1. God is not a deity who just lit the blue touch-paper and retired. Everything that exists, be it a cosmic egg with a possibly indistinct start point, or our world today, depends on God. Genesis 1 is not providing an alternative to scientific discoveries, but is teaching theological truths about the purpose of the physical existence of the universe (see also Question 9). At the start of the Bible we are given guidelines of approach as we seek to know what sort of being God is. It shows that the universe is not somehow an emanation of God, or a part of God, but that he is distinct from it. Should we worship creation? No, says Genesis. It gives us the revelation that God is distinct from his world, yet caring of it (for other insights, see Question 25).

'What place, then, for a creator?' The Christian reply is found within the pages of the Bible after Genesis 1.

Genesis is not meant to be a scientific text, and neither is the Big Bang theory meant to be a theological one. It is the scientific unpacking of the truth of Genesis 1:1, but the theory is neutral when it comes to the question of whether there is a God. If we still look for a reason as to why the Big Bang happened, then it will be found beyond physics. Genesis 1 has stood for two and a half millennia as a theological attempt to provide the foundations of what is beyond science.

Sum-up

● The Big Bang model explains observations which indicate that the universe must once have occupied a small volume that exploded outwards overcoming gravitational attraction.

● It doesn't make too much difference if a start point of space and time cannot be uncovered, though Genesis 1 and observation both suggest one. The Bible rather records the importance of God's continuing care in upholding creation in being.

● The statement 'God created the universe' is not a scientific explanation but a theological insight in accord with science. Genesis was not written as a scientific text, nor is the Big Bang theory modern theology.

12. Scientists can say how the universe expanded from just after the Big Bang without God being invoked. Surely he is a rather lazy God!

When it was discovered that we live in a dynamic universe arising from the Big Bang (see Question 11), scientists began to ask what was happening in its earliest moments. What were conditions like then? Such extreme conditions would have to be mimicked in experiments to get some insight as to what might have happened.

Experiments conducted in high-energy physics try to do this. These involve the bombardment of very energetic subatomic particles with each other. The results of such collisions have given a detailed understanding of the earliest moments of our universe. At its very earliest moments the temperature would have been colossal. In a universe 10^{-43} seconds old (1 divided by 10^{43} – 1 followed by 43 zeros – called the Planck time) the temperature would have been of the order of 10^{32} degrees C, and the whole universe would have had a radius of 10^{-35} metres, far smaller than a single atom's nucleus!

Under such conditions it is thought that the <u>four forces of nature</u> would have been effectively a single force. As the universe expanded and cooled they became the separate forces we experience today. This separation process has been partially verified by experiment. Within a fraction of a second, it appears that matter came together to form the constituents of atoms. <u>Quarks</u>, the building-blocks of atoms, were formed and combined together such that, at around a millisecond into the process, stable protons and neutrons (that make up atomic nuclei) were created. These then combined into simple nuclei of atoms after a few minutes. Lending weight to this hypothesis, this so-called <u>Standard Model</u> of the constituents of matter predicts from this process exactly the correct amounts of hydrogen (~75 per cent) and helium (~25 per cent) actually found in the universe. The formation of atoms and the inexorable effect of gravitation subsequently led to stars being formed in which nuclear fusion reactions could begin. The process towards life had started in the expanding universe.

I've outlined the model in some detail for a specific reason. The power of the model may lead us to think that we have an 'explanation' of what happened and that God is somehow redundant. The processes and the forces involved when we trace causation backwards in time seem to be a seamless whole. An evolving creation appears to generate its own processes and fundamental forces. What role then is there for God?

Creation appears to generate its own processes and fundamental forces. What role then is there for God?

As we look back into the early history of the universe it is easy to imagine that these unfolding paths are inexorable. As the forces of nature separated and the matter we see today became stable, we might wonder whether any changes in the way the universe grew would have had any effect. Was creation an uncontrolled roller-coaster ride permitting everything to unfold? The answer appears to be that it most certainly was not. We look back at what appears to be a wide path of development, but in going forward in time it appears to be more like a tightrope.

For example, the formation of stars requires that the force of gravity (versus the strength of the <u>electromagnetic force</u>) needs to be exactly the strength it is, otherwise typical stars like our sun would not burn for billions of years. Any variation would either lead to a 'damp squib' that never gets going, or to a star that goes into overdrive. Both would last only a few million years – insufficient time for life to begin. Our sun will potentially burn for around 10 <u>billion</u> years. Consequently, life has been given a remarkably stable and enduring environment in which to develop.

The material that forms us comes from stars that have burned out and exploded. We are made from stardust! But not any old mix of stardust will do. In the formation of the chemical elements inside stars by nuclear fusion, there is a 'fortuitously' favourable reaction for the manufacture of carbon, but a lesser one leading to its destruction. As a result this increases the proportion of carbon in the universe, making it higher than in other possible scenarios. These arguments about such 'coincidences' are often called <u>anthropic</u> relationships (in Greek *anthropos* means 'man' – see also Question 13). They indicate that the origins of the universe leading to our existence were very precise. Processes that some scientists see as limiting God's choices severely can also be seen as the precision of God in action.

Processes that some scientists see as limiting God's choices severely can also be seen as the precision of God in action.

Professor Roger Penrose has asked just how precise the initial state of our fledgling universe must have been. He estimates that the creator got it right to an incredible 1 in 1 followed by 10^{123} zeros – more noughts than particles in the universe! There must have been very great care in selecting the starting state of everything if even the everyday mechanics we take for granted are to occur. He writes, 'What does this say about the precision that must be involved in setting up the Big Bang? It is really very, very extraordinary.'[9]

But with all that, is God lazy? Did he just 'light the blue touch-paper' and retire? Or, to put it another way, was the universe created functionally complete, and has creative power been wholly transferred from God to matter itself (see, for example, Genesis 1:12 that might suggest it to a sceptic)? Any attempt at natural theology (discerning God from nature – see also Question 4) is always liable to this 'god of the gaps' objection. If God is given as the excuse for a special event, then the objection is sustained, but if the order of creation exhibits no gaps, then the universe is self-contained and God appears not to be needed.

To the Bible writers this denial of God's influence would not be a valid statement – God is the cause of all, both directly and indirectly (Exodus 14:21; Isaiah 44:28). God's creation was described as very good; his work is perfect, meaning as complete as he wished (Deuteronomy 32:3–4). The Bible is clear that God has not written himself out of the 'script' as it unfolds. His will is mediated through creation in creative acts (Revelation 4:11). What Christians must beware, as C. S. Lewis noted, is inadvertently using God as the explanation only at particularly important and occasional creative events, while the rest just happens 'naturally'.

The Bible is clear that God has not written himself out of the 'script' as it unfolds.

St Augustine wrote in an essay entitled *The Literal Meaning of Genesis* that in the beginning all creation existed in the mind of God potentially, and was realised as creation unfolded in time and God's wishes were enacted. A split between instances of 'special creation' and God letting creation run its course effectively independently of his will, is an artificial and anthropomorphic divide. Both downplay God's assiduous interest in the universe. From the time of the earliest prophets, God is proclaimed as one who creates the stars as well as being concerned at the behaviour of his created beings (Amos 5:6–15 is a good example). We may retire, but God never tires (Isaiah 40:28).

There will always be gaps in assigning scientific causes, or else science would end. Yet the division between natural and supernatural is not biblical. The best science can say to describe any particular event is that it is 'highly fortuitous'. The believer will say it was 'meant'. To one a single route appears without divine action; to another it is a path defined by the will of a loving God.

Sum-up

● High-energy physics has given vast insight into the intricate mechanisms leading to the universe that we see today.

● The processes of nature may often appear causally

complete, but science has discovered that this is not any old universe.

● The Christian insight is of a God who, in his grace, wills and enacts specific outcomes in history that appear simply improbable to those without the eye of faith.

13. The universe is so big. How can anyone believe we are of any significance at all?

If we look up into the night sky its vast expanse might lead us to wonder whether we are just insignificant specks in the vast distances of space. There are almost countless stars in our universe, some 100 <u>billion</u> in our own galaxy (the Milky Way) alone. It forms part of a group (called the Local Group) of galaxies, itself part of a bigger cluster. There are around 100 billion galaxies in the known universe. In view of such colossal numbers, how can we be of any importance to a divine creator, confined as we are to this little corner of space?

Size and significance are not inextricably linked, of course. Yet as scientists have studied the universe, a strange insight has begun to dawn on those who might not usually think about God at all. It seems that in order for living creatures such as us to exist, a universe as massive and old as ours, and as highly populated with stars, is in fact needed. At earlier times complex intelligent life could not have existed, while later the universe will not be conducive to life existing as we now know it (see Question 14). The ideas are summarised by a set of statements called the <u>Anthropic Principles</u>. Proposed by some British and American scientists, these have provided useful insights into answering the question of whether we are significant after all.

We currently believe that the universe is around 15 <u>billion</u> years old, give or take a few thousand million years (see Question 11). That length of time is needed for an initial generation of stars to be formed and die (often in explosive events called supernovas) and in that process make some of the heavier elements, of which we are composed, by nuclear fusion. New stars such as our sun were then formed as a second generation, and matter came together to form the planets we see today. Like good wine, our universe needed time to mature.

Like good wine, our universe needed time to mature.

Scientists have asked whether the universe would be the same if the fundamental constants changed slightly, such as relative values of the <u>four forces of nature</u> (see Question 12). One such force is that of gravity. Suppose that at the instant of the Big Bang the value of the force of gravity had been slightly larger than the value we experience. The expansion of matter would then have been prevented and the whole universe would never have escaped the force of gravity. The life of this expanding universe would have been over almost immediately, as matter, radiation and space itself were pulled back into a point again, like a collapsing balloon.

Now suppose the force of gravity had been smaller at the Big Bang than it is now. Then a universe would have been formed, but the force of attraction would have been too small and the resulting universe too dilute to enable galaxies to form. Such galaxies would not be able to provide the seedbed of life. It turns out that the forces have to balance in the simple model outlined above within a phenomenal accuracy of 1 part in 10^{60} (1 followed by 60 zeros!). Although other factors might modify the value, this degree of exactness seemed somehow 'meant' to the scientists who investigated it. It also became clear that many other balances were necessary to ensure that life developed. It is these extraordinary sets of circumstances that form the basis of these cosmological Anthropic Principles.

There are several forms of the Anthropic Principles first discussed by physicist Brandon Carter (see also Questions 18 and 44 for others). The least controversial is the Weak Anthropic Principle. This states that we should only expect to find values for physical and cosmological quantities in our universe that are in accord with us being here. This does little more than restate the observation of the anthropic relationships that we are not in any old universe, and it leaves open the question of a creator God's existence. The Strong Anthropic Principle goes further into <u>metaphysics</u> by saying that the universe is constrained to be as it is so that it will produce intelligent life. In other words, the universe is purposeful. We are then more than merely fortunate to be here; we are somehow meant to be here.

We are more than merely fortunate to be here; we are somehow meant to be here.

Have scientists found God? Before Christians give a cheer that some scientists are at least thinking about God, several cautions should be expressed, for the majority of scientists are wary of accepting the existence of purpose in the processes of creation.

There are several ways people can avoid the conclusion that a divine purpose exists for our world, and that God created the earth and subsequently humankind in his image (Genesis 1:26). They can remain agnostic and maintain that these anthropic balances are merely fortuitous. Alternatively, they can say that many universes have existed and so replace purpose (which dangerously hints at God's existence) with chance. Perhaps, they suggest, such previous universes had different values of physical constants or even different prescriptive mathematics as their basis (see Question 8). Our universe is then seen not as the result of anthropic design but as just the one that happened accidentally to be able to create life. Conceivably other universes exist elsewhere, some with life, some without, but we can't see them because of the effects of the Big Bang background radiation (see Question 11). Such radiation would also block out evidence of potential past universes (see Question 14).

Most scientists don't like theories with no evidence to back them up. Hence others have tried to reduce this level of anthropic exactness in another way. Maybe our universe isn't *that* special, they suggest, and so then neither are we. In 1979 American physicist Alan Guth suggested that in the very earliest moments of the universe, it went through a massive expansion which almost instantly blew up the universe from a subatomic size to thousands of kilometres across. He called this process inflation. Across the sky, features such as the background radiation are generally very smooth, which is what rapid inflation would produce. Guth's model explained how the balance of gravitation and expansion might appear just right. Rapid expansion then caused the universe to become both even and finely balanced without recourse to purpose.

Unfortunately for these scientists, inflation is itself a process that requires exacting conditions. Inflation needed to start and cease at just the right moment (at around 10^{-34} seconds into the lifetime of the universe). It also

required the existence of strange particles that had gravitational effects that were repulsive rather than attractive. In a later inflationary model, 'empty' space itself
had to have its own available energy! In other words,
fruitful conditions which are conducive to anthropic
arguments are still needed to explain the evolution of
the universe.

The presence of these anthropic 'coincidences' creates
a strong case for suggesting that we are significant.
Intelligent beings are not the end product of arbitrary
accidents in a pointless cosmos. Even if we accept the
idea of many universes, the existence of a creator is still
possible. God may have decided to create a manifold of
universes so that our inflationary one could arise.
Apparent chance does not implicitly invalidate the possibility of design; indeed, it may provide the opportunity.

The presence of these anthropic 'coincidences'
creates a strong case for suggesting that we are
significant. Intelligent beings are not the end product
of arbitrary accidents in a pointless cosmos.

These principles focus clearly on the strict conditions
needed for life to occur. Their existence is readily
explained by those who believe in a God who created us
amidst the countless stars as creatures who are precious
in his sight (Psalm 36:7).

Sum-up

● The universe needs to be this old and vast to enable
  us to exist.

- Size and significance don't always go together.

- Several coincidences exist which suggest that our universe is special, and they strongly indicate that there is a purpose behind it.

14. Christianity is about hope for the future, yet the universe is either going to end with a crunch or fizzle out. Where is the hope in that?

Science and Christianity do not only meet in confrontation over creation and the first book of the Bible. They differ in an understanding of events at the end of creation too, given in the last book of the Bible. Big Bang cosmology (see Question 11) not only gives a start point for the universe but suggests what may happen at the end of all things too. An early model by astronomer Alexander Friedmann suggested that depending on the amount of matter in the universe, either space would go on expanding for ever, towards eternal dilution and a 'Big Chill', or else gravity would win and the universe would end in a massive pile-up, a 'Big Crunch'.

Both events would not happen for billions of years according to the model. But which is more likely to occur? However, even if there were an exact balance in the forces, the universe would slow but never quite stop expanding, and life would experience a slow rundown. The balance condition where this occurs is called the Critical Density.

Discovering which side of the dividing line our universe is on has proved a problem. Counting all the stars we can see only gives us a few per cent of this Critical Density. However, the vast age of our universe, its structure and its undoubted fruitfulness imply we should be somewhere near this balance. The motion of galaxies, though, suggests that we only see a small fraction of the matter that exists (the non-luminous stuff is called 'dark matter'), and so this value can go up to maybe 10 per cent locally. Looking further afield to clusters of galaxies, this approximately doubles, but does not increase by enough to reach the critical value. The search is currently underway to discover where this proposed missing mass might reside. Elusive particles called neutrinos that only weakly interact with matter appear a good possibility. Observations on certain exploding stars in late 1998 suggest the universe may well still be accelerating after the Big Bang.

Either way, the future of the universe doesn't seem very optimistic for anyone (even if this universe were a part of some endless cycle, it turns out that future universes are unlikely to be as <u>anthropically</u> fruitful, getting nearer the conditions for the 'Big Chill'). We may ultimately explore this universe in space travel, but the Preacher of Ecclesiastes got it right when he said that all hope for things in this universe is in vain (Ecclesiastes 1:2). Of course, if you follow seventeenth-century Dutch philosopher Baruch Spinoza or some New Age thinkers today and claim that the universe is part of God or maybe is God, then this is terrible news too. All things, including God, will pass away one day!

For a Christian a different scenario is on offer. St Paul agrees with the Preacher when he says: 'If only for this life we have hope in Christ, we are to be pitied more than all men' (1 Corinthians 15:19) – but then he points to another ending.

The Preacher of Ecclesiastes got it right when he said that all hope for things in this universe is in vain.

Long before the end of the universe our own death

will come. Death is a necessary part of this life. Every minute some 16 million cells in our bodies die and others are being formed through division to maintain our shape (nearly!) and to eliminate any damaged cells. If this programmed cell death, called apoptosis, does not function correctly, then cancers and other diseases can result. New life, in biological terms, needs death as its precursor. A similar hope is presented in the Christian faith. In Christ we move from death to life, says St John (John 5:24). St Paul says that although in Adam all die, in Christ all shall be made alive (1 Corinthians 15:22). Yet can this hope be more than pie in the sky? It can be, for it is an inescapable consequence of the resurrection of Christ (see Question 41). The disciples staked their lives on more than just a nice idea or a lucky shot; it was an <u>empirical</u> event.

The disciples' hope was not just to survive death, but to become like the risen Christ. The resurrection was not resuscitation, but to be part of the new creation vindicated by God. The resurrection of Jesus was a foretaste of what was to come (1 Corinthians 15:20). Since Christ took his humanity into the presence of God, then we too are offered the hope that our humanity, suitably sanctified, will also be able to come into the presence of holiness. This belief does not mean that God somehow made a mistake in making us as we are, but that the good in people is redeemable by God. The new comes out of, and is built upon, the good of the old. Just as my body cells are replaced in this life, a process that maintains the same 'me', so my person, with all its strengths and weaknesses known to God, will be ultimately redeemed (Job 19:25–27) as part of the Christian hope of renewal.

The disciples' hope was not just to survive death, but
to become like the risen Christ.

Of course we don't know how all this will come
about. Christianity is not a 'reasonable religion' in the
way that some in the eighteenth century wanted it to be.
Religions and science both have their <u>axioms</u>, beliefs
that must be taken somewhat on trust. But faith means
trust. Many scientific axioms are given the benefit of the
doubt each day, if only because they work and appear
self-evident. For Christianity this axiom of future hope
is based on actual evidence, and is neither self-evident
nor religious pipedreaming (1 Corinthians 15:6).

The new heavens and earth are not described in the
Bible in order to encourage abstract <u>metaphysical</u> speculation, but to urge Christians to examine their lives
because an end is in sight. It is not accidental that the
start of the Christian year is Advent, just before
Christmas, which asks probing questions about the
choice of lifestyle we make. The theme and challenge of
Advent is built upon the hope that the God of redemption will not forget his creatures and that what he has
created will not be lost for ever (Revelation 21:3).

Sum-up

● The tussle between the forces of nature will lead
either to a Big Crunch or a Big Chill in billions of
years' time. All will be vanity if we hope only for
this world.

● The Christian hope is centred in a God who will not

abandon what is good in the creation that he has made but who, in the resurrection, gives us a hope of a new creation (Luke 19:10).

● Advent is about being ready for an end that will inevitably come for each of us in death, affecting how we live in the expectation of eternal life.

15. Isn't it arrogant to say that God made the universe with us as the pinnacle of it?

'Do not think of yourself more highly than you ought,' recommends St Paul (Romans 12:3). But for all his small stature in the cosmos, mankind has often done so. We view the world and the stars beyond it from a human perspective and with our own agendas. The Bible is concerned with how God revealed himself to his people, and therefore also has this human focus. Yet in certain places, such as Psalm 104, it gives a greater vision of the God who made the heavens and earth. It reminds us that God delights in the whole of his creation too. It follows the psalm in which the writer remembers that we are but dust (Psalm 103:14)!

We view the world and the stars beyond it from a human perspective and with our own agendas.

Evolutionary history, culminating in mankind (*Homo Sapiens*), was not a straightforward path of consistently advancing complexity (see Questions 23 and 43). Rather, from our perspective it was as tortuous a route as the Israelites took getting to the Promised Land. A series of geological and environmental changes led to successions of creatures dominating the fauna. For example, at the end of the Permian era some 240 million years ago, movements of the earth's crust led to a single landmass given the name Pangæa. Resulting desert conditions and global warming led to the extinction of all but the smallest shrew-like creatures. From mammal-like reptiles the lineage to mankind emerged, but before this happened the dinosaurs held the stage. Through a process of evolving complexity, punctuated by geologically rapid clearing of the earth, mankind eventually arose.

We should recognise, then, that our cosmic surroundings are not merely a backdrop for the affairs of humanity. The Lord rejoices in all his works (Psalm 104:31), and mankind, late on the scene, is only a small part of them. This does not mean that we are of no significance, however. We can affect and have certainly affected our own planet to such an extent that the need to cease damaging activities is becoming urgent. We have the potential to create cataclysms similar to those of the past (see Question 42). Adam was given the job of tilling the Garden (Genesis 2:15) and we retain that responsibility of wise husbandry.

Our cosmic surroundings are not merely a backdrop
for the affairs of humanity.

Some people have an adverse view of religion because of the instruction to subdue the earth (Genesis 1:28). The Hebrew word 'subdue' (*kabash*) is a strong word, reflecting the hostile world of nature the people of the day knew of then, and that the third world knows today. But it was also used of King David's conquests (2 Samuel 8:11) and of the order imposed by Joshua (Joshua 18:1). Kings could bring order or chaos, but they were still answerable to God. Alongside this mastery, God calls us to care for the land and its animal life. Destruction of wildlife and exploitation and exhaustive farming of land are forbidden (Exodus 23:11). The covenant of Noah is for both mankind and animal life (Genesis 9:9–10).

Even though we might be more valued than the grass (Matthew 6:30), God values both flora and fauna not merely for goodness in some narrow instrumental sense, but more importantly because all creation has intrinsically good elements that give delight and glory to the Almighty (Psalm 145:5).

Unwittingly, science often exacerbates human exploitation because of its approach to the environment. Nature becomes a thing out there to be dissected and studied by our minds. Consequently, the sheer wonder of creation can fade with this analytical approach. Philosopher Marilyn Frye has labelled these two views as the 'loving eye' and the 'arrogant eye'. The latter takes an independent view, standing aloof and using or subjugating creation as it wishes. It does not see the goodness that the loving eye of God sees.

Unwittingly, science often exacerbates human exploitation because of its approach to the environment. Nature becomes a thing to be studied.

The opposite of subjugation is not submission, however. We need not become refugees from modernity. Theologian Sallie McFague has remarked that this view only continues the domination with roles reversed. Neither should we have to go so far as to consider the earth as a living organism (often called Gaia after a pagan goddess) in order to respect our environment, for it is not alive (though life and auto-regulating systems exist on it). We should rather re-evaluate nature as being a product of God's creativity and not simply as an object for our pleasure. Rural people often understand this symbiosis, and get angry with city-dwellers who regard nature as a commodity for their use, usually wanting it to remain as an unchanging idyll.

The loving eye recognises others' needs, and good stewards need to have a responsible and responsive understanding of the processes of nature. This is not nature worship, but a proper care and concern for other life. We neglect nature at our peril. We may well be at the pinnacle of creation, but the only way from there is down, through a fall. The outcome of that is something that needs addressing by assessing the consequences of the lifestyles we choose (Philippians 2:12). It has been addressed by God too in seeking to offer us salvation (see Question 40).

Sum-up

● To their shame, religions have often taken an instrumental view of the universe.

● Science, by its methods, all too readily objectifies and devalues nature.

● A proper purpose and place for nature is to see it as loved by God, and to be respected by both scientific investigators and theologians.

16. Aren't there parallel universes where the consequences of different decisions we make are followed?

We expect our world to be transparently understandable down to its roots. But science has been surprised this century by findings that refute what seems common sense. At the atomic and subatomic level the continuous view of nature is wrong. Energy comes in packets called quanta, and small particles, quantum particles, behave contrary to the way things do in our large-scale world. Such behaviour is described by quantum theory (also called quantum mechanics).

Quantum theory provides us with a description of the foundations of the universe that cannot be determined with complete accuracy. When Laplace suggested that a complete description of the universe at one instant would enable us to calculate the future precisely, he was wrong (see Questions 4 and 26). At its roots our universe is 'fuzzy', and has a reality that can never be completely unveiled but is provisional (see Question 2).

Quantum theory is a bit like a lottery. It is inherently about probabilities, not about certainties. In the macroscopic world something is either in one place or another. It cannot be in both places at once. In the quantum world it can be in either or in a mixture of both these places at the same time! All small subatomic particles like electrons and photons (particles of light) behave in this way. An experiment called the double-slit experiment shows this nicely. In this experiment the quantum particle can go through a barrier with two slits in it. If we specify the particle as an electron, say, then the spaces between the rows of atoms in a crystal provide suitably spaced slits.

Quantum theory is a bit like a lottery. It is inherently about probabilities, not about certainties.

If we have a detector on the other side of the crystal, then only one signal is recorded at one point for each electron going through the system. Yet the pattern built up over time at the detector is identical to that which would result if the particles were replaced by waves. At certain points you will never record the electron because the electron 'wave' interferes and cancels out, just as two waves can 'cancel' each other's effects when a peak from one wave coincides with a trough from another. An interference pattern results. In fact, even if only one electron is sent through the system at a time then the resulting pattern is exactly the same as if many had gone through. The electron has gone through both slits at the same time!

Quantum things behave as both particles and as waves – you can do experiments showing this dual nature. Your television and computer 'chips' would not work if it were not so. This *unpicturable* wave/particle duality in nature is inherent for all quantum things, but as the size of the particles increases, this dual nature effect becomes minute and our familiar patterns of 'normal' behaviour result.

Scientist Werner Heisenberg discovered that the reason for this duality is because we cannot have detailed knowledge about quantum particles in the same way that we might have about larger ones. So at one moment you might know where an electron was, as if it were a particle, but then you wouldn't know where it was going. Again, you might know where it was going, but then you would be uncertain where it was, like a wave. Think of a wave front breaking along a beach – there's no one point at which it does break, but many. This Principle of Uncertainty governs all quantum behaviour. It makes the quantum world indeterminate. It is an inherent property of microscopic behaviour – not because we can't do experiments that are good enough.

Now of course the quantum world and the macroscopic world interact when measurements are made. But if the electron in the experiment can be anywhere, like a wave at one instant, and then suddenly it is recorded somewhere at the next, like a particle – what is happening? Physicists call this the 'measurement problem'. No one quite understands what happens, but the electron wave effectively collapses to one point on the detector. There is a discontinuity – the electron is everywhere, and then in the next instant somewhere, where it is detected. But what about those places on the wave front where it might also have turned up? As in a lottery we have a winner, but what about the other participants? Are they only virtual winners?

One solution to this conundrum is the many-worlds hypothesis. It suggests that the particle reaches all positions, but that the detector is the place of the discontinuity. I record the photon at one point, but there is another 'me' in another *parallel* universe who records it at another point and so on for an infinity of worlds.

This strange hypothesis, originally by Hugh Everett III, is favoured by many cosmologists who want to do justice to the mathematical equations (see Question 8), but would like to avoid the idea that a wave instantly becomes a particle as a result of the detector which observes it. Yet despite its strangeness there is little doubt that quantum theory is well-nigh correct. It has been verified to a great degree by experiment, although gravitational theories cannot at present be reconciled with it, and relativity doesn't quite fit with it either. Here in this created universe is something that defies scientists – in fact physicist Richard Feynman has said that such attempts at explaining are going down 'blind alleys' of comprehension.

Consequently, is there in fact another world where you did win the lottery (given that another 'you' might go in for it)? Alas, we have no way of discovering these alternative worlds, nor can we ever have. They are as unrealisable as the dreams of winning the lottery are when the hopes of millions collapse as the real result is drawn.

The many-worlds hypothesis is not liked by many scientists. This is because, whether they acknowledge God or not, the purpose of science is to try to explain the rationality of this world within its natural confines. This hypothesis appears untestable, and therefore beyond the realms of science. It requires far less of us to say that there is one world, a world of chance created by one God, than to believe in a constantly splitting reality. It seems simpler to suggest that any outcomes that are not observed in our universe don't happen at all, and hence retain a solitary, perplexing world. Without it human ethics becomes artificial, and human freedom becomes an illusion if all decision paths we take exist, albeit in different parallel worlds. The Christian gospel of grace and forgiveness testifies that the decisions we take are real and are ones that we are responsible for in this single if strange world (Leviticus 5:17).

Those who think that the revelations of religion are contrary to common sense have to reconsider their view in the light of apparently nonsensical quantum discoveries. Like the oldest and wisest who put down their stones first in John 8:9, it is those who recognise that the implausible does happen who may be more open to God. Our reliable world is built upon strange but apparently necessary foundations (Isaiah 55:8).

Those who think that the revelations of religion are contrary to common sense have to reconsider their view in the light of quantum discoveries.

Sum-up

- Quantum theory is about the behaviour of small things, which differs from our common-sense understanding of the behaviour of the macroscopic world.

- The quantum world is described by probabilities, and it is not determinable in the same way as our mechanical world of cause and effect.

- The many-worlds notion tries to picture this by suggesting that the universe splits to eliminate this uncertain aspect. In each universe a real result is obtained. However, this view makes greater demands on its adherents than faith does on those who believe in a creator God!

- If the criterion of common sense is used to deny the possibility of God, then it is rocked by the sheer nonsense of the extraordinary atomic world.

17. Isn't everything that exists a unity and, in fact, God?

Albert Einstein didn't care for <u>quantum</u> theory. Experiments which showed that matter at the atomic level has a dual character, behaving like waves in some experiments and as bullet-like particles in others, alarmed him greatly. In that realm it is necessary to deal in probabilities, not in certainties. By contrast, the big world deals with certainties like position and velocity. Those who play ball games can accurately judge the trajectory of a ball in order to catch it, for example (see Question 16). But for a quantum particle you cannot know both position and velocity together; this pair of variables (and some other pairs too) cannot be determined with total accuracy. At its roots the quantum world is not 'set'. Einstein hated this idea of probability and unreality. 'He [God] does not play dice with the world,' he once said. There must be properties hidden from us that would mean these particles were really like the macroscopic world we are all familiar with.

'God does not play dice with the world,' Einstein once said.

In 1935 Einstein, together with Boris Podolsky and Nathan Rosen, challenged the scientific community with a hypothetical experiment (called the EPR experiment from their names) looking for these hidden variables. A later interpretation expressed it in terms of two quantum particles that have interacted. By quantum reasoning each should retain an influence on the other, and whatever happened to one should instantly influence the other. Einstein didn't like the idea of non-localised behaviour, because his <u>Special Theory of Relativity</u> said that nothing, including signals from one particle to the other, could go faster than the speed of light. This quantum behaviour was instantaneous, almost spooky, action at a distance. It was like something out of the *X-Files*! Einstein wanted something localised and real, like the ball, like ordinary objects we see each day.

In 1964 physicist John Bell was able to show mathematically that if there were hidden properties for any quantum particle then there were also limits on how localised any particle's influence could be. In 1982 Alain Aspect was able to test the EPR idea by ejecting two photons (particles of light) from a single calcium atom. From a measurement on a property of one, he determined that the other, which was separated from it, was influenced *instantaneously* by the measurement. In 1997 Nicholas Gisin and colleagues at Geneva were able to separate particles by six miles and still show this immediate interaction!

Einstein's challenge was met. If he wanted to keep the observation that no information could be communicated faster than the speed of light, then quantum 'spookiness' was the true reality in the universe! Einstein's follower, David Bohm, tried to keep some sort of common-sense reality by suggesting that particles could then be perceived as the 'peaks' in a sea of interacting waves. His quantum ideas, although unable to be reconciled with <u>relativity</u>, have survived. He viewed existence as comprised of what we see and measure scientifically (he called this the *explicate order*), and a holistic fabric of reality that formed its basis (the *implicate order*).

This interconnectedness of things may make us wonder whether everything isn't now interconnected with everything else. The idea that 'All is one' is the basis of a philosophy called monism. It dates back to the Greeks, but it has resurfaced regularly in various philosophies and in Eastern religions. It claims that everything is related, interconnected and ultimately one and the same. Many versions are tempted to identify this unity with God. Diversity, monists claim, is only an appearance; in fact, monism asserts there is ultimately one great ocean of being. Matter and thought are two manifestations, even illusions, of the one reality. Scientist Max Born even thought that the quantum world was subjective and unreal. His idea has Mahayana Buddhist overtones, in which the existence of anything is solely dependent upon relationship.

Interconnectedness does not, of course, imply that everything is the same. Bewilderment in physics shouldn't lead us to dissolve the rationalisations we have made over who or what we are, or indeed who God is. Tradition and experience are still good guides to what is so, even if they cannot be regarded as absolutes in a post-Newtonian world. Interconnectedness doesn't deny reality, for the results of quantum experiments are as real and predictable as Newton's classical ones, and as amenable to mathematical description, if not quite so picturable. The nature of quantum reality that physics describes is not an undifferentiated unity – quite the reverse. It is a highly structured world that has precise properties.

Interconnectedness does not, of course, imply that everything is the same.

Christians should avoid going down a monist road that leads to everything being regarded as one. Usually this road leads people ultimately to champion either matter (in materialism) or mind (in idealism). We affirm a God who has created a physically objective and real world, but we must admit that absolute determinism isn't possible. The freedom of will that we believe God has given us is perhaps a reflection of a freedom that he has intrinsically given to his creation at its fuzzy quantum roots.

Our presence in the universe as observers alters the state of what is observed (see Question 18). At the quantum level this is intrinsically far more important than at the macroscopic level. But we should beware importing quantum ideas into the macroscopic world, just as Einstein was mistaken in trying to do the reverse. A new mysticism based loosely on what happens at the atomic level is unlikely to be in harmony either with Christianity or most scientific practice.

A new mysticism based loosely on what happens at the atomic level is unlikely to be in harmony either with Christianity or most scientific practice.

St Paul warns Christians in Colossians (Colossians 2:8) against being captivated by ideas like monism. The real world is built up of quantum particles, but it is not reducible to their behaviour. Chemistry is built upon the laws of quantum theory, but its reactions are real and quantifiable. The foundations of a building may tell you a little of what the building may be like, but they will not tell you everything about it.

Sum-up

- Experiments have shown that in the quantum world strange non-local effects do exist.

- This interconnectedness is only one part of nature's fabric, which as size increases merges seamlessly with the familiar Newtonian physics of our everyday world. The physics of the quantum world is, however, mathematically structured and quantifiable, and not some undifferentiated whole.

- Monistic beliefs based loosely on what happens at the quantum level are unlikely to find agreement either with Christianity or most scientific practice.

18. Modern science is finding out that the world of the atom is very strange. Maybe Christianity isn't the whole truth?

Science is based on observation. Its knowledge is *a posteriori*, knowledge gained from experience. Before the eighteenth century, theories of reality were based largely on *a priori* knowledge, which is knowledge derived from reason alone. Philosopher Immanuel Kant attempted a synthesis of these approaches with a theory that recognised that our minds form the theories and yet also need experience of the world around. Minds impose a framework such that the reality we build, Kant said, is not reality as it is, but only as it appears to us. He also tried to resolve potential conflicts between religion and science by recognising the existence of two worlds: the phenomenal world, which is accessible to experiment, and the noumenal world, which is what we can conceive of with our minds, but not perceive with our senses. He placed God in this latter world, a world of faith. The splitting of these worlds has enabled scientists to work within a philosophical framework that religion could not challenge. It has, in consequence, marginalised faith so that it seems irrelevant to many today.

Kant's ideas have enabled scientists to work within a philosophical framework that religion could not challenge.

Kant would have been both fascinated and worried

by the <u>quantum</u> world. Here observations make things happen. Occurrences are dependent on events being experienced by people. In our double slit experiment (see Question 16) the presence of a detector 'collapses' the quantum entity which is behaving like a wave, making it respond as a particle. Another example is radioactivity. Some atoms are particularly unstable and decay (break up), yielding radiation such as alpha, beta or gamma rays. We cannot predict when any particular atom is going to decay, but only say how long it will take for a certain proportion of atoms to decay. The time taken for half the number to decay is called the half-life.

In the quantum world observations make things happen.

Any individual atom can then be said to exist at any time in a condition (a mixture) of both having decayed and not having decayed. In the classical (Newtonian) world we see events which have definite causes (see Question 7). Yet that classical world is made up of bits of the much smaller quantum world. At what point, therefore, do the worlds connect?

Scientists love to do thought experiments. One is called Schrödinger's Cat. Suppose, said scientist Erwin Schrödinger, a cat is locked in an isolated box, along with a radioactive source. If an atom of the source decayed, then it would trigger a device that released poisoned gas to kill the cat. At any time an atom is in a state that can be correctly described mathematically as being both decayed and not having decayed. So the gas is both released and not released, and the cat is in a (quantum) state of being both dead and alive! The quantum world apparently affects the real world directly.

When we open the box and look, the quantum world instantly collapses to one result. The cat can only be either dead or alive in the world we experience. We ourselves seem to have made the difference. Some theologians have suggested that at last here is a suggestion that mankind is important in the scheme of things. We are necessary in order to bring about reality through being observers! This *participatory* <u>anthropic principle</u>, suggested by scientist John Wheeler, appears to give us a reason for existing. Did God create the world, yet need us to make it real?

This is a nice idea, but mankind appeared rather late on creation's stage. It seems a little presumptuous to suggest such a major role for human consciousness. Yet in 1710 Bishop George Berkeley suggested that material things are fabricated by the mind. Things are real, he said, because they are perceived. He added that things unperceived by man were still real because they were in the mind of God.

This might seem rather attractive, except we might hope that we are more than just the dreams of God. His sustenance of the world consists in giving to all creation a measure of true independence (see Question 45). We are then free to co-operate with God. For things to be as they are there is a logical necessity even for God to respect the integrity of his own creation. God must create true freedom, or true justice and mercy could never exist either (Isaiah 30:18).

Experiments in the quantum world have been a reminder to scientists that the world they inhabit is affected by their presence. We cannot completely separate the world into observer and observable, noumenal and phenomenal. Quantum theory reintegrates our view of the universe. It appears that our own dynamic participation in the affairs of the universe is important. Yet in stating this, we must recognise that the universe is a balance between interconnectivity and distinctiveness. Kant and Berkeley each have only partial solutions.

Quantum theory reintegrates our view of the universe. Our own dynamic participation in the affairs of the universe is important.

The problem with the cat experiment is that the quantum world isn't like ours. We assume that all events have sufficient reasons for determining outcomes and here there are none that we can see in this experiment. Theologian Nancey Murphy has followed Berkeley's ideas partially and has suggested that with no hidden variables (see Question 17) *God* provides the sufficient reason to move the world on and collapse the wave function. God's role is as the hidden observer and 'variable', working in all quantum events for which the rest of his universe provides a necessary backdrop.

It appears, then, that what is happening in the quantum world is much more than something being made real by us. Even today, though, scientists are just not sure how the big and little worlds fit together. It seems we just have to live with this world of complementarity, and accept the wave/particle roots of nature.

The Christian faith isn't meant to be a set of philosophical statements but one rooted in the physical world. The Christian view is that material reality does matter because God bothered with it. This follows from the creation and is reinforced by the incarnation of

Christ (see Question 40). We should be humble before our Maker in consequence (Job 11:7–8). Science too needs a proper humility, which some of its better exponents in the quantum field have recognised. Wolfgang Pauli, who proposed why all atoms were stable, liked to answer those who assumed that one day science would explain everything by pleading that there be 'no credits for the future'.

Sum-up

- The counter-intuitive world of quantum theory makes it plain that we are an integral part of the universe and cannot make it an independent object of study. We are not, however, living in a world which is the product of our minds.

- Faith should not be an escape into another world. God is very much interested in this one.

- Both science and faith should be humble before assuming that we can fathom everything.

19. Is it possible that one day a scientist will write down an equation that explains everything about the universe and then there will be no need of God or religions at all?

At various times during the past century researchers have wondered whether there are any more giant leaps to be made in science. In the mid-nineteenth century the discovery of the way light propagates unified the fields of optics and electromagnetism and encouraged physicists to wonder whether that was the end of physics. They thought that only a few problems were left to be sorted out. But within a few decades Einstein had shown with his Theories of Relativity that the idea of absolute space and time no longer held true. It also led to the discovery of quantum theory (Questions 16–18). Reality was like peeling an onion, and layer after layer was being uncovered.

The quest for an equation that explains everything, a Theory of Everything (often termed a TOE), is an example of science being rather presumptuous. Stephen Hawking, in his bestseller *A Brief History of Time*, suggests that philosophers have not been able to keep up with scientific developments. A TOE, he suggests, would enable us to answer the question of why everything exists. If we could, he said, *'then we would know the mind of God'.*[10] Christians realise that this search for meaning is implanted by God into people so that they will seek him (Ecclesiastes 3:11). As St Augustine once wrote, 'For you made us for yourself, and our heart finds no rest until it rests in you.' There is nothing sinister, therefore, in mankind knowing something of the mind of God (e.g. Psalm 34:8); indeed, he has enabled us to do it in some small measure and to glimpse his ways (Isaiah 40:13). A rather more modest goal of physics has been to attempt to produce a means of explaining why the various fundamental constants (such as the value of the charge on an electron), which don't seem explicable in terms of simpler things, have the values they do.

The quest for an equation that explains everything, a Theory of Everything, is an example of science being rather presumptuous.

Actually what is meant by a TOE is usually rather more like this limited goal. It attempts to unify the different aspects of the universe rather than explain 'everything'. For example, the <u>four forces of nature</u> are probably a manifestation of the same force (see Question 12). At the universe's earliest moments we know for certain that two of the four forces of nature, <u>electromagnetism</u> and the <u>weak force</u> which governs radioactive decay, were one and the same. So there could be a theory or theories that will unite all these forces into one – a *Grand Unified Theory*. Without bigger particle accelerators than we have at present, it is impossible to test these ideas, although the behaviour of matter around <u>black holes</u> may assist our understanding.

Saying that these theories 'explain' everything is a bit like saying that the physics of a vibrating string 'explains' the orchestral works of Beethoven. In a narrow descriptive sense it does, but not in many other ways that include instruments and orchestras and musical appreciation. A TOE might be self-consistent, but it would not be self-explanatory or mathematically complete (see Question 8). It would just restate mathematically (and in a more limited way) the spiritual question 'Why is there anything rather than nothing?'

Saying that these theories 'explain' everything is a bit like saying that the physics of a vibrating string 'explains' the orchestral works of Beethoven.

A new theory that attempts to be a TOE is called the '<u>superstring theory</u>' (actually several have been suggested). Superstring theory suggests that all the forces and matter we experience are different manifestations of the vibrations of tiny 'strings' rather than of points. All the various <u>quantum</u> particles that have been found experimentally can be logically grouped in this way.

These strings are so tiny that around a massive 10^{21} of them would stretch across the nucleus of an atom. The mathematical picture suggests that prior to the forces of nature separating and mass becoming distinct at the Big Bang, the universe was a strange entity of ten-dimensional space that split into four and six dimensions. The symmetry 'broke' and four became three-dimensional space and time as we know it, and the other six are somehow curled up and we cannot see them! In the face of such proposals belief in God looks, in comparison, to be quite reasonable!

Scientists often employ two contrasting arguments against God's existence. The first is to claim that everything is ultimately simple and therefore it is more likely to occur without the need for a complex God. The second is to say that all is complex, but the mind behind must be more complex. So why make life more difficult by bringing in the idea of God? However, TOEs breed new complexities, such as the existence of these hidden dimensions, which deny the first supposition. Complexities are hidden within the fruitful laws of TOEs, and we often fail to recognise them. Although God created the universe in a highly symmetrical state, it was far from simple (see Question 44). In the evolution of the universe the simple precedes the complex, but within that simplicity is the potential for the complex emerging.

With regard to God's complexity, we must realise that God is not some additional component of the universe; he is its external author (Isaiah 29:16). Arguments which suggest that the possibility of complex things arising spontaneously is less than for simple things in the material universe are invalid for God. God is not a *material* part of his creation. In fact, as Keith Ward points out, God has an 'integrative' simplicity because many happenings make much more sense once we acknowledge his presence.[11]

The several superstring theories cannot be resolved at present and they appear to be interrelated. Recently it has been suggested that there is a twelve-dimensional all-encompassing mathematical theory which has been dubbed the 'F theory', with F standing for Father. In Ephesians 4:5–6 we read of a religious revelation that lies beyond science, of 'one Lord, one faith, one baptism; one God and Father of all'. Christians already have a theory of everything: a Father theory which is grander than any unified theory that human reason can fathom (John 1:1–4). Theories of everything point clearly to a complex world, rational to our conscious minds, and point to a Mind behind it.

> Christians already have a theory of everything: a
> Father theory which is grander than any unified
> theory that human reason can fathom.

Sum-up

● A Theory of Everything tries to explore the coherent unifying principles within nature, both for matter and forces.

● We cannot reduce metaphysics to physics – we will still be asking, 'Why does anything exist at all?' Theories of everything just frame the big questions of life in different ways.

● Such ideas do not point inevitably to an atheistic worldview, but are sympathetic to a theistic one because they point to a universe that appears inherently explicable.

20. If life on other planets is found, then surely our special place in God's sight, which the Bible talks about, is blown away!

In August 1996 NASA produced meteorite evidence that seemed to point to the past existence of primitive life on Mars. It led to a furious debate as to whether fossilised bacteria remains were present in the sample. No definite conclusions were reached but it aroused fresh interest over whether 'little green men' do exist. Just how likely is life in the rest of the cosmos? Our feelings of being 'special' are surely at risk!

Writing an equation to determine the number of intelligent, communicable civilisations in the universe isn't too difficult, but getting a meaningful answer to it is. One multiplies the rate at which stars form (which is roughly known) by the proportion which have planets. Multiply this by the proportion of those that are amenable to life starting and the proportion of those on which intelligence will emerge. Additionally, the effect of the proportion of those that manage some kind of interstellar communication, together with the length of that civilisation, must be taken into account. This is known as the Drake equation. The problem is that no final result can be guessed at with any certainty. Guesses of anywhere from one planet with life (obviously at least one!) to a million for our own galaxy have been given, depending on the enthusiasm of the scientist for or against ETI (extra-terrestrial intelligence).

Most calculations have to assume a 'Principle of Plenitude' (a suggestion by A. O. Lovejoy); that is, what is possible will occur. In other words, since our solar system doesn't look very different from others, then life might be expected to evolve in a rather similar way in similar situations. Our sun is a typical star and we know of more than a dozen planets, including one small solar system, around neighbouring stars.[12]

If life is commonplace in the universe, where does that leave the notion of man made in the image of God? Many ideas have been forthcoming down the centuries as to what this metaphor of 'image' might mean. Relationship, morality, self-awareness and consciousness are some suggestions. God's revelation and above all the incarnation of Christ seem to point powerfully to a very special relationship between people and their creator. Yet mankind never warrants the totality of God's attention (see Question 15). He delights in his non-human creation too (Job 38), even, presumably, including life on other planets. Even though he may offer mankind a unique relationship, it is not an exclusive one.

Even though God may offer mankind a unique
relationship, it is not an exclusive one.

Indeed, God viewed everything he had made as very good (Genesis 1:31). It had a harmonious beauty of which mankind was merely a part. However, the biblical message is that mankind is special precisely because he is a 'fly in the ointment'. Disobedience has led the Father to seek the prodigal son, not because of how good the son is, but because of how gracious the Father is (Luke 15:11–32). Mankind needed a rescue package because he was made in the image of God, and we are precious in his sight (Isaiah 43:4). In that sense we are special in the whole cosmos in being rebellious creatures!

Although some decades ago people felt that there must be millions of civilisations across the galaxy, attempts at sending or listening for messages recently have proved fruitless. Scepticism has led people to re-evaluate the early optimistic conclusions of Drake's equation. Something of the special circumstances involved in the possible *uniqueness* of mankind in our galaxy, and even the whole universe, has been high-lighted by other leading scientists (see also Question 13).

For example, the story of life on earth has been by a series of extinctions of certain species and the subse-quent development of others (see Question 43). In the case of dinosaurs, any subsequent evolution would probably not have led to a large brain developing. Their ancestors, crocodiles, have developed over 200 million years, yet although they effectively occupy a niche in nature, they have not developed oversized brains as humans have done. Their cold-blooded metabolism is thought to have prevented it.[13] With our warm-blooded internal thermostats, our brains are able to function in a stable metabolic surrounding, although they consume a colossal 20 per cent or so of our bodily resources. This poses a profound challenge for any purely evolutionary theory of descent to explain (see Questions 23 and 24).

If we compare this development with the forty or so basic designs for sight that different forms of life cur-rently use, we might realise that intelligence as a charac-teristic is at a premium, both globally and potentially universally. The evolution of intelligence is not some inevitable end product of cosmic chemistry. It is the presence of our <u>anthropic</u> world and its own history that has contributed to our appearance.

Evolution of intelligence is not some inevitable end product of cosmic chemistry.

Furthermore, with the expansion of the universe the number of suns like our own that are coming into being is falling dramatically. The majority of the stars in our galaxy suitable for life are older than the sun by several billion years. Therefore Nobel prize-winning scientist Enrico Fermi suggested that if aliens existed, they would already be here! Even in our short civilisation we have been able to send probes out beyond our solar system. If others had time spans of billions of years more to do this, shouldn't we see them already? (Of course they may have found us in past eras and decided to stay well clear.)

Having no evidence, of course, is not the same as having proof that there is none. But the searches for ETI have been scaled down of late, and the 1997 movie *Contact* criticised this. We might well find other intelligent life (see Question 21), but in the meantime we might realise that the message of the gospel to a special world from its creator is in consequence also likely to be very special. For those who follow our Lord already, his commission is clear and we must follow his last vital command on earth in Acts 1:8: 'But you will receive power when the Holy Spirit comes on you; and you will be my witnesses in Jerusalem, and in all Judea and Samaria, and to the ends of the earth.'

Sum-up

● It is almost impossible to predict whether any

life, especially intelligent life, exists on other planets. The biblical message is that God the creator cares for all life.

● With the failure to find extra-terrestrial intelligence, scientists have been looking at the way mankind developed, and have realised that we are more special than they previously thought.

● God thought we were worth saving, and that is the good news for his world.

21. If intelligent creatures are discovered on other planets, will they need saving too?

Even opposing scientific hypotheses can be used to attack religion! Some say that intelligent life is so overwhelmingly improbable that planet earth is some freak abnormality in a vast universe. Therefore it is unlikely that there is a creator interested in a minority of living creatures. Others have suggested that there are many worlds like ours, and that the whole cosmos is brimming with life (see Question 20). Surely, then, such creatures will have other spiritualities that render our own faith either obsolete or at best just one among many? Either way, salvation looks a purely local human affair, and of little importance!

However, this becomes an important issue when we declare that this creator God was born as one of us two millennia ago in a Roman backwater *for us men and our salvation*, as the Nicene Creed puts it. Is Christ merely the solution to the unique problem of human disobedience? Does the King of kings being born in a stable show us just how alienated we all are from the Holy One and his creation? C. S. Lewis wondered whether the vast distances in space were some divine quarantine precaution to prevent other races discovering us![14]

Does the King of kings being born in a stable show us just how alienated we all are from the Holy One?

Of course we cannot tell. We have only one data point in the cosmos at present when it comes to counting the creatures that can discern God's presence. Other creatures on earth do not appear to have this ability in the same way. We do not proclaim the gospel to our dogs. My spaniels prefer retrieving tennis balls – that is their way of delighting their heavenly Boss. The book of Job contains a wonderful picture of God's delight at his creation. Other life presumably does the same, on whatever planet it exists.

Yet two theological answers emerge when we ask whether other life that is in some way 'spiritually aware' needs saving. One is to conclude that salvation is God's business and we can assume that he would have found other ways to save creatures that are unknowable to us. Some aliens might not have fallen from grace. But what if they have? Have there been countless equivalents to Calvary? The second answer suggests that there is only one Good Friday, but it has the power to redeem all creatures, both known and not known to us.

In fact the Bible does address this problem, albeit indirectly. The New Testament writers faced a debate over whether Gentile believers could join the predominantly Jewish church. Today, with our history of racial awareness and concern for equality, this debate might seem strange to us. But the Jewish apostles were amazed that God could be reaching out to *alien* Gentiles (Acts 15:12). Surely God would have nothing to do with such unclean people? Paul wrote his letter to the Galatians specifically to show them how God always meant to include them, and that a Jewish Saviour could save Gentiles. It was a vital point that had to be made, otherwise Christianity would always be a minor sect in Judaism. Christianity was to be a global faith inaugurated by *one* event of reconciliation (Hebrews 9:26). Christ was not *a* solution of salvation but *the* solution for the world.

The Jewish apostles were amazed that God could be reaching out to *alien* Gentiles.

But was Christianity meant to be a faith for other worlds? At the start of John's Gospel and the letter to the Hebrews we have a partial clue to the answer: 'Through him *all things* were made' (meaning Jesus, the Christ; John 1:3). Hebrews 1:3 puts it this way: 'The Son is the radiance of God's glory and the exact representation of his being, sustaining *all things* by his powerful word' (my italics). In the Eastern church this universal nature of Christ has been emphasised historically more than in the West.

St Paul writes to the Colossians about this universality too. In the first chapter he says of Jesus (verse 15): 'He is the image of the invisible God' – the image of God whom we cannot see. The Jews were forbidden to make any image of God, for it was bound to deceive. But Paul says that Jesus is the physical image of God that cannot deceive, and that if you want to know what God is like, then look at Jesus. That is the universal claim that Paul is making. Verse 16 goes on still further: 'For by him all things were created: things in heaven and on earth, visible and invisible, whether thrones or powers or rulers or authorities; all things were created by him and for him.' In verse 17 Paul says, 'He is before all things, and in him all things hold together.' This cosmic Christ is the source of coherence in the whole universe!

This cosmic Christ is the source of coherence in the whole universe!

The power of God for salvation, then, is for *all who believe* (Romans 1:16). Jesus' salvation goes beyond Jews to Gentiles and affects the whole creation (Romans 8:19–23). Paul hints that the universe is waiting for the redemption of our race. He is talking to earth-bound human beings, but his perspective is universal. The cosmic shepherd has other sheep and sheepfolds (John 10:16). The goal of the grace of God through the cross is to have one flock and one shepherd (Ephesians 1:10).[15] The effects of that one event in space and time will be universal when God's nature will be seen by all at the end of history (1 Corinthians 15:28). History will then be seen properly as 'his story'.

Science fiction often reflects more on our behaviour than that of other creatures. For example, *Star Trek* characters like the Ferengi and Romulans hold a mirror to us – Economic Man and Imperialist Man. Innocent aliens would do well to steer clear of this solar system! God could not but reveal his loving, self-giving, cruciform nature to other spiritual creatures, just as on 'first contact' we will inevitably betray our true nature. For fallen creatures going their own violent way, Christ is the solution to their self-destructive alienation from God. As Asian evangelist D. T. Niles said about the Christian faith: it is one beggar telling another beggar where to find bread.

God could not but reveal his loving, self-giving,
cruciform nature to other spiritual creatures.

Sum-up

● The biblical message of salvation burst its Jewish
confines in the early church to go to alien races that
did not know God.

● Christ is portrayed biblically as the one through
whom everything was made and in whom the whole
creation hangs together.

● Christ is the universal redeemer offering God's salvation and reconciliation across all time and space.

EVOLUTIONARY HEADACHES
Primordial slimes and chance events

22. Life on earth arose from chemicals accidentally joining together. Surely that shows that God is neither loving nor nasty, but just indifferent.

Magicians are very clever people. With sleight of hand they lull you into not watching what is really going on. They have a hidden agenda. You may think that science is done impersonally, but you'd be wrong. Scientists are human beings, and human frailty and sin can never be entirely eliminated from their work, even though they present an objective image to the outside world. Beware believing all the conclusions of science uncritically; most scientists don't.

In the heady days of the 1950s and 60s it was thought that science could answer every question, including those about the origin and nature of life. Around the time of the discovery of <u>DNA</u> and the molecular basis of reproduction, experiments were conducted to try to mimic the chemical processes that led to life. These experiments simulated the supposed atmosphere of the earth some 4 <u>billion</u> years ago, a billion years after the earth's probable formation. Owing to high volcanic activity, the earth's atmosphere then would have consisted of gases such as carbon dioxide, ammonia and other gases, but little oxygen.[16] In 1952 Stanley Miller set up such an 'origin of life' experiment. He mixed selected chemicals and water in a flask and used an electric spark to simulate lightning and provide an external energy source. After a week he found a mess in the flask which contained molecules called amino acids, the components of the replicating molecule DNA in all living cells.

Several scientists jumped on the bandwagon and photographs of them were taken peering, god-like, into chemical flasks. They designed various starting conditions and got different amino acids when the experiments worked, and horrid oils when it (mostly) didn't. But the impact was tremendous; a start had been made. Surely the jump to creating life was now shown to be small and therefore statistically very likely? It appeared that chemists could at last play God.

Several scientists jumped on the bandwagon and photographs of them were taken peering, god-like, into chemical flasks. It appeared that chemists could at last play God.

Unfortunately, all chemical reactions are reversible to some extent. Doctoral students in organic chemistry learn just how hard creating new molecules is, but they also quickly realise how difficult the extraction of their newly created molecule is. If they don't extract it, then either the reverse reaction or other reactions take place. Both break down the precious product. The art of organic synthesis needs careful design, and usually a lot of trial and error. Miller designed his experiment; the chemicals he used and the proportions he used them in were no accident.

Production of the complicated self-replicating molecules needed to create life requires a great deal more than watery primordial soup. The latter is quite good at producing some simple molecules, but unfortunately the water breaks down complex molecules like proteins made of amino acids. Other scenarios were therefore suggested. For example, it was proposed that formation is aided by surfaces such as clays, and even ice, but no breakthroughs were made.[17]

Production of the complicated self-replicating molecules needed to create life requires a great deal more than watery primordial soup.

Yet today the philosophical implications of these failed experiments still elicit religious scepticism. Why should we bother with God if his influence is not really needed at the beginning of life? All that is needed is a soup of chemicals and a lucky break! Perhaps it was not DNA but RNA, or some other simpler replicating precursor, that started it all off, resisting reverse reactions and not needing a divine chemist. All you have to do is wait long enough, and anything is likely.

The problem is that this last statement may well be untrue. Theologian Keith Ward calls it rather indelicately 'the fallacy of cosmic promiscuity'! Scientists simply cannot tell whether life on earth is a product of accident or design because they don't know the actual processes that occurred. They only guess at mechanisms that are far simpler than the incredibly complex self-interacting chemistry of living cells today (see Question 24). There may or may not have been enough time for this chemistry to establish itself without any guidance – we just can't tell.

It is not true that all you have to do is wait, and anything is likely. This view has been called 'the fallacy of cosmic promiscuity'!

Although little experimental progress has been made, it is still tempting for sceptics to try to reduce the likelihood of design by other means. For example, a mathematical argument is sometimes employed. We know there are around 10^{20} (a hundred million million million) stars in the known universe, and many may have planets revolving around them. Although the formation of life by accident might be improbable, the sheer number of planets might lessen the odds. It's like someone having lots of goes at a lottery; eventually one attempt should win. All one has to do is suggest (and it *is* a suggestion) that the likelihood of accidental life is less improbable than around 1 in 10^{-20}. Hence the conclusion follows – life developed by accident! Yet against this one could argue that God's design automatically included so many planets as an essential part of the universe he created, so that the goal of life *was* reached.

We shouldn't frown upon these 'creation of life' experiments. They were a good idea, for as molecular biologist Michael Behe noted, if they hadn't been done we would have no idea just how difficult and unlikely this process might be. Atheists could have waved their arms and implied that it was easy, but we now know it wasn't. Christians too will recognise from these results the magnitude of God's care for us.

It is important to realise that when some scientists suggest life is an 'accident', they are saying something that is beyond the limits of science to comment on. Producing an estimate of how improbable an event is cannot confirm or deny the likelihood of God being its author. But when we suggest that life is not an accident, we too are saying something beyond science.

Producing an estimate of how improbable an event is cannot confirm or deny the likelihood of God being its author.

Sum-up

- Experiments on the origin of life show that the process is far from straightforward or simple to reproduce in the laboratory.

- The level of improbability of the processes involved is largely unknown, so science cannot really comment on whether or not the formation of life is accidental.

- In suggesting life is not an accident we are saying something that is beyond the limits of science, although science may restrain what we can say.

23. Aren't we the products of a 'mindless' evolution that Darwin discovered?

Apart from the Galileo incident (see Question 5), the chief battle fought between science and religion has been over the theory of evolution of <u>species</u> by means of natural selection. It was first published in Charles Darwin's book of 1859, *The Origin of Species*.[18]

Darwin based his thesis on extensive observation over twenty-five years. It was already recognised that life was varied, but the ways in which such variety developed were not understood. During his voyages in the Beagle from 1831 to 1836, Darwin noticed that isolated populations of particular species showed slight variations in behaviour and body shape (this 'outer creature' is termed the <u>phenotype</u>). He had read an essay by Thomas Malthus on how natural limitations (of food) would inhibit population growth, and formed the idea that species develop by slow and gradual changes of individuals in successive generations. Beneficial changes would favour survival and subsequent reproduction. Cumulative changes, termed *natural selection*, would cause species to evolve.

This gradualistic approach in science was much in favour at the time. From about 1800, geologists such as Charles Lyell and William Smith had begun to recognise that rock formations developed from a gradual sedimentary process. The fossils in them showed changes in fauna and indicated that the earth was old. There had been many extinctions and appearances of distinct species. Also, the older rocks showed simpler creatures. Some sort of change in them must have occurred over time to match the gradual environmental changes. One might question how God could have constructed a *good* creation of unchanging species if they would become less suited to their changing environments over time. Morphological likeness between species, and the presence of redundant vestigial organs in some animals, also needed to be explained.

Darwinists who are antagonistic to religion state that in the mid-nineteenth century the church uniformly believed that the world was created in 4004 BC, from a literalistic and chronologically strict reading of Genesis. This is not the case.[19] All but one of the authors of the famous *Bridgewater Treatises*, essays that in the 1830s discussed God's design of nature, favoured a geologically old earth. Earlier, the Church Fathers, including St Augustine, had found theological truths in an allegorical interpretation of Genesis 1 and 2. It was not that the biblical message was unimportant, but that there was more than one literary device used in it to convey truth. It had also been suggested for several centuries before Darwin that there was a 'gap' implied between verses 2 and 3 of the first chapter of Genesis, between God creating a 'formless' earth (meaning essentially unproductive) and then instilling fruitfulness by his creative word. There appears to have been a deeper recognition before Darwin that a 'young' earth simply didn't feel right.

It was not that the biblical message was unimportant, but that there was more than one literary device used in it to convey truth.

Other suggestions put forward included the far-fetched one that fossils were created by God to give an 'apparent age', or that the Hebrew 'day' in Genesis 1 could refer chronologically to millennia or epochs. The latter idea is suggested by some today.[20] People had been considering how biological change might have occurred, but Darwin provided the first coherent and evidenced answer.

People had been considering how biological change might have occurred, but Darwin provided the first coherent and evidenced answer.

Darwin's ideas met with some initial approval by the church, and several evangelical friends such as Professor Asa Gray in the USA promoted Darwin's hypothesis. There were also many scientists who did not share his views of gradual change, for in the previous century Carl Linnaeus had suggested that species were separate and no gradual development had occurred. Unfortunately, the genetic basis for selection had not been discovered, although, in central Europe, August-inian monk Gregor Mendel was in the process of doing so (see Question 24).

Conflict over Darwin's theory grew, culminating in 1860 with the famous debate between vigorous Darwin supporter and atheist Thomas Huxley and the Bishop of Oxford, Samuel Wilberforce. Wilberforce had been briefed by Richard Owen, first Director of the Natural History Museum, who didn't care for Darwin. This appears to have been partly because Darwin was rich, and science was a hobby rather than employment for him. Impartial verbatim reports have not survived, though it is known that both the scientist and the bishop thought they'd done well. Huxley and his followers later intensified the debate as one between evolution and creation partly because of their dislike of ecclesiastical power.

As in Galileo's day the science was not sufficiently advanced to make a stronger case (see Question 5). Scientific opponents attacked the church for both valid and invalid reasons. Theology and faith suffered in consequence, and the conflict and polemic worsened as the century wore on. The fact that many devout men agreed with some of Darwin's suggestions was lost, and the richer picture of God that they suggested was obscured.

The medieval picture of a static ladder of creation had ignored the real dynamic processes of nature. This wrong <u>paradigm</u> needed shifting. The biblical phrase 'God created . . .' says little or nothing of mechanism, but much about divine purpose. The created world by default was previously seen as the unchanging backdrop to human history. Now Darwin's thesis included all living things as part of God's creation. All that God made was very good (Genesis 1:31) and 'good' meant fit for the purpose, with the potential of adapting and improving within a dynamic universe.

The medieval picture of a static ladder of creation had ignored the real dynamic processes of nature. This wrong paradigm needed shifting.

Both Darwin and the Bible dispel the deist concept of God being an absentee landlord, aloof from the events of the world. God's sustenance of creation means more than just supervising it; rather it demonstrates a steadfast love in allowing the fruitfulness of <u>anthropic</u> laws to unfold as a reflection of his will. God is known in renewing processes and change. He is not a petrified idol of the past, but the God of the present (Luke 20:38).

God is known in renewing processes and change. He is not a petrified idol of the past, but the God of the present.

Two issues are important as we consider Darwin's ideas. The first is the place of chance in this process. Darwinism is about the struggle for survival with limited resources. Changes resulting from random genetic <u>mutations</u> have been conclusively demonstrated to cause phenotype changes. This does not mean that the changes are blind, for they are not isolated from the consequences, including the existing environment. Changes that occur need to produce a viable new individual or they are literally dead ends. Both genetic change and environmental interaction work such that the overall evolutionary process is non-random. Both stability and random events are needed to avoid either an unfruitful chaos or an unchanging static world, both of which lead to extinction. Life takes a path of increasing complexity which is built into the whole unfolding fabric of creation. Novelty that can arise and respond to a changing environment provides a route for increasing complexity. The emergence of sentient creatures becomes a real possibility which culminates in us. Purpose is enacted through this. Those who ascribe evolution to 'blind chance' use the words not in a scientific but in a <u>metaphysical</u> way, implicitly and illegitimately denying God's existence.

The second question is whether Darwinism is the total explanatory factor in the evolutionary emergence of new species. Now we know that Darwinian evolution on the small scale does occur. It has been observed in the changing camouflage of English peppered moths and in adaptive changes in sizes of finches' beaks. But can Darwinian gradualism explain all the complexity of life on earth? Many do not think so (see Questions 28–30).[21] Other processes have been suggested (see Question 24).

Novelist Charles Kingsley supplied a partial answer in marrying a purposeful process with a strong element of chance when he suggested that God's greater wisdom was seen not in making things, but in making things make themselves. God's indirect causation can be recognised as life develops within an <u>anthropic</u> universe; the expensive luxury of consciousness being at the pinnacle of it (see Question 13).

God's greater wisdom is seen not in making things,
but in making things make themselves.

Darwin himself was a sensitive Victorian gentleman in every sense of the word. His conclusions of a nature 'red in tooth and claw' horrified him. The death of his ten-year-old daughter Annie in 1851 (in an age of high juvenile mortality) badly dented his trust in a loving God. The gradualist mechanisms he defined seemed to leave little place for God to work functionally in the world as a direct cause. Natural selection as Darwinists see it has no bias, no lure towards the delightful, nor towards even the sentient, the altruistic or the religious. Only survivability counts. It is a gloomy picture of

despair if that is all there is. No wonder Darwin apparently lost his faith.

Christians see the world in a much more positive way,
as the product of a good God's creativity. The world is
not solely comprised of the most ruthless and prolific
Darwinian creatures. If it were, it would be a world
without beauty or value. Yet this doesn't mean that the
Bible views the world through rose-tinted spectacles.
Both Testaments know the reality of death, but do not
see it as negating purpose in life. Sir John Polkinghorne
has said that this combination of joy and suffering
seems to be part of the 'package deal of the universe'
(see Question 36). Competition and struggle are part of
life in all its richness. It is one that God himself has
known in Christ too; and he is not indifferent to it
(Psalm 23:4).

Reading design into the processes of the world does
not prove the presence of a creator and sustainer, but it
is consonant with it. Randomness is part of the divine
means, a tool for exploring within the whole creation,
for which a directed purpose readily explains how the
beauty and complexity of life arose. What we cannot
live with, since Darwin, are theologies that picture God
in terms of the static views of the past.

Sum-up

● Darwin provided a theory of how competition for
  resources drove the process for adaptation, together
  with a mechanism for the development of species
  that were clearly somehow related.

● Supporters and detractors of natural selection were
  found in both scientific and religious communities.

● Natural selection does not describe a world that is perfect, but one that God made good, which means that it is fit for the purpose he intended. The out-working of chance and certainty provides the opportunity for God's purposes to be realised.

● Darwin did push Christian theology away from the view of a static creation, with God being used as a plug for gaps in our understanding, towards a dynamic view in which God still works (John 5:17).

24. I've heard some Christians say that evolution is a myth. For example, the eye is so complex it could never have evolved. Are they right?

In 1802 clergyman William Paley published *Natural Theology; or, Evidences of the Existence and Attributes of the Deity*. If you found a watch on the ground while you were out for a walk, he said, you'd assume from the intricacies of its functioning that there must have been a watchmaker; that is, a designer. This, he suggested, was also true for creation. Darwin then proposed a naturalistic solution (see Question 23) that appeared to involve no divine designer. Which, if either of these, was correct? Could Darwin's theory explain the undoubted complexities of creation?

Until this century Darwin's theory had little mechanistic knowledge to support it. Mendel's work on genetic inheritance provided the clue to the biochemical basis for the variations in successive generations that Darwin's theory needed. Each parent, it was found, supplied half the genetic material (from the parent cell <u>chromosomes</u>, which are composed of <u>genes</u>) for its offspring. These chromosomes were found in the nuclei of almost all living cells, and the nucleic acid components determined heredity and growth. In 1953 the structure of <u>DNA</u> with its double helix and the potential for self-replication was discovered, and thereby the mechanism for changes in creatures from generation to generation. DNA functions as the blueprint for building and maintaining the structures of the cell and indeed the whole organism.

Scientists combined these genetic insights and Darwin's ideas to produce a comprehensive picture of evolution they called Neo-Darwinism. Fossil information allowed a 'tree of life' to be built that was patchy but showed an increasing complexity and branching. Information about genetic and biochemical resemblances between living things showed that a virtually identical tree could be built from consideration of these similarities and differences. We share some biochemistry with even the simplest living creatures, but the nearer the relationship, the more similar are the biochemical reaction pathways. This is strong evidence for evolutionary change.

Yet the evidence also suggests modifications to Darwin's gradualism. Two such modifications that have been suggested are sudden extinctions (see Question 43), and the rapid emergence of new species after long periods of apparent stability. A novel proposal has also been made that the mitochondria, which act as energy suppliers in each of our cells, may be relics of symbiotic bacteria. We are beginning to realise that events other than gradual change have also been important in describing the history of life.

Even if we agree that Darwin's gradualism is not the complete story, we seem to have, nevertheless, a complete picture of how creation evolved naturalistically. This seems to leave no room for a designer – or does it? Consider how a designer works today. A modern designer usually doesn't make an item directly, but he works as part of a team (which often he has set up). He is the first and final cause of the object, in that what he wills is built, but he is usually only indirectly responsible for manufacture. He works with the assistance of a construction team, continually refining the design, improving and testing it to eventually make the final finished item. Real design is a dynamic process.

Often items are not designed from scratch. Designers take short cuts. Existing designs are incorporated into the new design. If the process calls for a step that can already be carried out by an existing mechanism, then this does not need designing again from scratch, although slight modifications may be needed. You build complex things from simpler components that already work. For example, car components such as gearboxes or clutches are used on different models. Also, off-site designers often leave it to on-site constructors to get the minutiae right. Within certain limitations and existing design codes, they produce something that is fit for the intended function.

Modern design methods seem to provide a far more promising analogy for creation than Paley's argument alone can provide. Such an analogy for creation seems more fitting than suggesting a once-for-all, almost magic event of divine labour. Evolution, then, can be seen as part of the larger construction set of creation within which natural selection plays a part.

Evolution can be seen as part of the larger
construction set of creation.

With this greater insight into the design process we can now see the creation of various species, which Christian theology has often seen as separate divine acts, as milestones for us in a continuing but not solely uniform process. Modern evolutionary theory does accept discontinuity in processes, such that a new species is defined as a separate population unable to interbreed with another species. They are often described as twigs on the tree of life.

Currently, retracing evolutionary convergence of this tree of life is proving a problem. Fossils of the earliest animals appear from around 570 million years ago (the Cambrian period), but within 25 million years all the main animal groups had arisen. This apparent 'Cambrian explosion' of activity is not readily explicable in Darwinist terms (although arguing from little or no information is usually dangerous – possible evidence of tracks of <u>billion</u>-year-old complex worm-like creatures has been recently uncovered, although this is disputed).

This apparent 'Cambrian explosion' of activity is not readily explicable in Darwinist terms.

One of the arguments against Darwin has concerned the evolution of the eye. All the components in it are needed if one is to see anything. How could they have come together all at once, except by design? Evolutionary biologists have looked at eyes in other living creatures. They have found a range of varying complexity that suggests ways in which the evolutionary process *may* have progressed. First of all a light-sensitive cell is needed. If cells are clumped together and are in a cavity, then some sort of directional information may be possible. If it is in a cavity, then a lens can increase the sensitivity. These tiny steps, it is proposed, are advantageous for selection, and build up a final complex eye, given sufficient time.[22]

But what if even the little tiny steps were themselves also highly improbable? Would we ever get off the foothills? Biochemistry professor Michael Behe[23] has suggested that between DNA and the whole creature lies a chemistry of evolution that is phenomenally complex and largely undiscovered. Behe has suggested that the biochemical processes are so complex that even these little Darwinian steps are unexplained giant leaps. The chemistry of even the simplest sort of light-sensitive cell (our first step above) is so intertwined with feedback loops and self-catalysis that it looks irreducible to simpler processes. He likens it to a mousetrap – either all the components work exactly right or nothing does; you can't evolve a mousetrap, you can only design one![24] Science may wish to avoid God as an explanatory device, but Behe suggests that we admit that we have no idea whether it is valid to replace the improbability of God with a large number of less improbable steps. However, we must be careful in seeking to bring God back as a direct cause that we do not create another 'God of the gaps'. God works in mysterious ways that may not always be improbable – we ascribe his work to all creation, not just parts of it.

God works in mysterious ways that may not always be improbable – we ascribe his work to all creation, not just parts of it.

In modern science quantum indeterminacy (see Question 18), chaos theory (see Question 26) and possible biochemical irreducibility identify more clearly the open weave of the fabric of reality that previous science seemed to have sewn up. How much these new insights give us in effectively uncovering intrinsic causal gaps, we're not entirely sure. They appear to be characteristics that allow an <u>anthropic</u> world to develop. Christians believe that both God and we have genuine freedom to act in the world (we certainly feel we do!). God's freedom may be seen both in the overall picture and by direct action. His working may be seen and understood by faith (Hebrews 11).

Sum-up

- Paley's arguments left an impression of a single designed event that made creation seem more like magic than rational construction.

- Design is a dynamic process working towards a final goal that can provide insight into how God creates.

- Evolution is one means by which God builds a good creation fit for the glory of God and giving glory to him.

- Arguing from design to God has proved dangerous in the past. We must recognise that science cannot, and indeed most probably will never be able to, close the causal web of reality.

25. If evolution has no place for Adam and Eve, then the start of the Bible is flawed. Why, consequently, should we trust the rest?

The opening chapters of Genesis (the name comes from the Greek word meaning 'origin') have often been described as mythical. This is often taken to mean that they are untrue. But theological myth is different. It is a means of conveying important abstract ideas in narrative form. In a scientific world, though, our criteria are somewhat different, and we are more concerned with the detail. What status, then, can we give these writings today?

The first thing to say is that by the standards of the day, the author or authors of Genesis 1 and 2 would be considered scientific in their approach. The whole basis of Genesis is to take creation out of the realm of the plaything of the gods, which is how neighbouring religions saw it, and to demythologise it. To assert that believing in the opening chapters of Genesis is equivalent to believing in fairies and goblins is to miss completely the points the author is trying to communicate.

By the standards of the day, the author or authors of Genesis 1 and 2 would be considered scientific in their approach.

In contrast to other creation stories of the ancient world, Genesis 1 is an attempt to look at creation dispassionately. Any idea of the material world being formed

146

out of dead bodies of gods (such as in the Babylonian creation story *Enuma Elish* where Marduk kills Tiamat, the chaos deity, and uses her body as material for the earth) is absent. Creation is the product of God's will, and not the result of heavenly squabbling. He is the creator, and accordingly the author of Genesis has understood that the universe has a value and a purpose.

Genesis is based on the insight that creation is a process. The text is not a result of joining together separate creation myths for flora and fauna and humanity, as other religions had. It asserts that all is one creation, an act of the one God. Genesis does not picture God creating the world by some instantaneous magic trick (though doubtless he could have). Without that insight we might never have looked for a process at all.

Genesis does not picture God creating the world by some magic trick. Without that insight we might never have looked for a process at all.

Two creation accounts are given. Genesis 1 begins from the creation of general requirements and moves to the specifics; Genesis 2 focuses on the creation of mankind and then adds the surroundings. These two perspectives should tell us to be cautious before we attempt to fit the scientific account into the pages of Genesis or vice versa. Such caution is often ignored. In the first verse of Genesis 1 the Greek idea of creation out of nothing is probably not in the author's mind, but rather the sovereignty of God as sole creator.[25]

The description continues with the creation of light and darkness, and the formation of dry land from the sea (as modern geology indicates). The objection is often raised that if Genesis 1 is meant to be a literal account, then the sun and stars are created on the fourth day (Genesis 1:14–19), long after the creation of light (Genesis 1:3). We can see that isn't possible, but the author of Genesis probably couldn't. The sun and moon aren't mentioned by name – they are demoted to being called greater and lesser lights, merely signs of the passage of time. It seems the writer wanted to make the then more vital theological point that sun and moon worship is wrong. They are created objects. The author did not wish to deify the heavens and the earth around him.

Creation is seen to progress from being a formless desert, incapable of sustaining life, to becoming dry land with plants, trees and living creatures created subsequently. A continuous but non-uniform process is in the author's mind; there are real new happenings that transcend what has been created before. What is created corresponds to what the author now sees around him. The livelihood of nomadic peoples and later settled farmers was dependent on finding and settling on lush pastures (the meaning of the word Eden). This is the finished picture that Genesis 1 and 2 paints of around 15,000 years ago. All creation accounts, both scientific and religious, seek to explain how things got to be as they are now.

A continuous but non-uniform process is in the
author's mind; there are real new happenings that
transcend what has been created before.

In the book of Genesis, mankind is created on the same day as the animals, and is linked with them in that male and female genders are created as well. Genesis talks of creatures in their 'kind'. Again, we should beware reading in modern concepts of class, species or other scientific classification of the living world. The author of Genesis does not write as a taxonomist so much as an observer of the world around. In the case of Adam and Eve, the names are often translated as proper names, but the Hebrew text uses the definite article signifying a common (generic) noun for Adam (until as late as Genesis 4:25 in the NRSV).[26] The usual Hebrew words for man and woman aren't employed generally because theological points are being made by the use of these names. The observation is given that the 'adam' is made from the ground (Heb. *adamah*), highlighting an undeniable mortality rather than one inherently divine. Also, in the account of the creation of woman out of man, the similarity of the Hebrew *is* (man) and *ishshah* (woman) is emphasised to reflect a common humanity and interrelatedness.

If we wish to do justice to Scripture we must recognise and respect its message. God's message was given first to people who were not scientists, but they could go beyond common thought to separate the world around from being at the mercy of supernatural beings. In the Old Testament, Israel often had to do battle with the foreign influences of those who believed in gods of nature (Deuteronomy 12:2). What matters is not so much whether Genesis gets its details exactly in accord with current scientific knowledge (although in comparison with other accounts it is remarkable how far it does), but primarily what it says of our relationship with God and each other.

Did Adam and Eve exist as real individuals? From a study of the genetic variety of human evolution from ape-*like* ancestors, at present it appears that *Homo Sapiens* was indeed derived from a single mother – an East African Eve, and perhaps therefore a single pair of ancestors. Fossil studies show a similar timescale for the emergence of mankind, with a separate branch much further back going to today's apes. A variety of near-human ancestors arose around 1 to 2 million years ago and spread throughout the world. However, modern man later developed cave painting, elaborate tools, burial rites and possibly primitive religious customs around 30,000 years ago. The genetic basis of modern man led to the final emergence of creatures with a propensity for faith, culminating after a period of time in religious practice, expressed in the revelation of God to Adam related in the Old Testament. Historically, adam (man) becomes Adam.[27]

In its literary way Genesis challenges its hearers to see that God is relevant to them since Adam is pictured as living in their area with similar lifestyle as a cultivator, rather like a medieval painting showing Christ born with surroundings contemporary to the period. Genesis is more in the realm of art than science, but nevertheless significant truths lie within it.

There are those who use the scientific account to dismiss the moral force of the insights of Genesis, and do not follow its insights about respect for the world around. There are others who are so intent on defending the truth of the details of Genesis that they fail to convey its message to the world. Both are unfortunate roads to go down, because there are still people today who want to worship the earth or the sun, or who see themselves as incipient gods. The theological battles of Genesis have not gone away. Genesis is a giant leap away from superstition and points towards a rational universe that has structure and integrity. To say it is flawed misunderstands its literary genre and its genius, and we neglect its purpose at our peril.

Genesis is a giant leap away from superstition and points towards a rational universe that has structure and integrity.

Sum-up

● Genesis is an attempt to distance creation from ancient stories and points towards an objective understanding of our origins.

● Genesis recognises the interrelatedness of all creation just as modern science does.

● Genesis describes a creation process that took time. This reflected the patient care of its creator. But in this process creature and creator are kept distinct.

● We should beware exceeding the truths Genesis seeks to convey by reading modern ideas into it, but nonetheless should recognise and revere its inspired genius and message.

26. With a big enough computer could we predict everything, and so have the mind of God?

The British love to talk about the weather. It is so unpredictable that sometimes all four seasons seem to come within just a few days. Indeed we expect its unpredictability, and when an anticyclone gets stuck over the British Isles and the weather remains hot, dry and sunny for days, people begin to hope for a change!

Before this century, and despite the weather, the laws of nature were believed to be held in the straightjacket of <u>determinism</u>. Newton's laws of motion and of gravity seemed to provide a complete account of how a body would behave under the influence of external forces. Hence there should always be precise evidence of what causes anything to happen, and everything from the motion of planets to personal decisions should in principle, if not always in practice, be totally predictable. This view, championed by Pierre Simon, Marquis de Laplace,[28] seemed to be beyond dispute.

Before this century the laws of nature were believed
to be held in the straightjacket of determinism.

However, scientists now recognise that the real world is often not that simple. Generally, in order to discover what underlies events, scientists need to restrict the parameters of a particular experiment to make sure that known variables, such as temperature or pressure, remain constant. This avoids outside factors interfering with results. They also often simplify their models so that they become easier to solve.[29]

However, most of the world frankly is not like this. In forecasting the weather, a system which is far from equilibrium, it was found that predictions from even simple models using deterministic equations like Newton's were often inaccurate. This was because even small uncertainties in the magnitudes of certain causes could lead to massive changes in effects. This phenomenon, found by meteorologist Edward Lorenz, was called the 'Butterfly Effect'. A butterfly flapping its wings in Brazil could change the path of a hurricane in Florida! The prediction of weather for a day ahead might be reasonably accurate, but over longer periods the predictions depended heavily on knowledge of the initial conditions being extremely accurate.

Some scientists realised that this behaviour, which became known as chaotic behaviour, was widespread. It was not due simply to the complexity of the system (though that doesn't help in the case of the weather), but was an inherent property of the mathematical laws that govern or describe the system. Small variations in forces could act like levers to produce large and unpredictable events.

Despite its name, chaos theory is not about disorder. Laws do not necessarily form a straightjacket for behaviour, but often they do determine boundaries, and they can, of course, produce ordered and stable outcomes.[30] But often within such boundaries, and under certain conditions, even the tiniest of inputs can cause a large response.

Laplace used his ideas of a determined world to link cause and effect irrevocably. He termed it the *Principle of*

Sufficient Reason. That meant that no divine input was ever needed as a corrective. As a consequence, we tend to think of order and disorder, or certitude and uncertainty, as being mutually exclusive. But chaos theory indicates how both may be found within any system, be it the weather or an evolutionary system. Chaos theory counters earlier assertions that with a big enough computer, using a snapshot of the world now, we could work out what the future holds. Chaos theory and quantum theory (see Question 16) make it clear that we cannot build a reliable 'crystal ball', and that Laplace's machine-like universe is a fiction (at least it doesn't adequately describe our universe). Some scientists are beginning to realise that there are limits to what we can know.

We cannot build a reliable 'crystal ball', and Laplace's machine-like universe is a fiction.

A few scientists have suggested that this behaviour is symptomatic not merely of our ignorance but of the fabric (the <u>ontology</u>) of reality itself. Scientific study almost takes it as a tenet of faith. In the case of <u>quantum</u> mechanics this seems so. It is suggested then that within the universe there is an openness that allows a real if limited freedom. Deterministic laws will limit action, but do not always totally constrain it. And with that possibility comes a partial answer to the question of whether we are truly free in our thinking. There are all kinds of factors (or possible causes) that enable us to reach decisions, but chaos theory suggests that we can still decide freely. Indeed, if events in our brain gave us no choice and led to criminal actions, we would not in any fundamental way be responsible for them.

Deterministic laws will limit action, but do not always totally constrain it.

This dichotomy between freedom and determinism can be seen in the Bible. There are texts that suggest God is in control of his universe absolutely. Proverbs 19:21: 'Many are the plans in a man's heart, but it is the Lord's purpose that prevails.' But equally there is also a real call to make a decision for God, such as that in Matthew 18:3: 'And [Jesus] said: "I tell you the truth, unless you change and become like little children, you will never enter the kingdom of heaven."' True repentance appears to be a contrast to determinism. Yet chaos theory shows us that physical laws can permit true freedom, even within tightly set systems. Consequently, the true steadfast love of God can allow us to respond freely to him (see also Question 45).

Sum-up

- Chaos theory describes real world systems that can be very sensitive to external influences; they are inherently unpredictable.

- Chaos theory suggests that the future is open and we do have real if limited freedom. Therefore no computer could accurately predict the future.

- Because we are not Laplacian robots, our freedom and God's freedom may not be illusions.

27. Hasn't science now demonstrated that there is no such thing as an immortal soul?

In St Luke's Gospel, Mary goes to visit her cousin Elizabeth who is expecting a son (John the Baptist). Mary's hymn of praise to God is recorded for us in Luke 1:46–55: 'My soul glorifies the Lord and my spirit rejoices in God my Saviour.' Did Mary think she was referring to different parts of herself by these words, as if she were composed of soul, spirit and body? In fact her words echo part of Psalm 35 (verses 9 and 10), where soul and bones are mentioned. The Hebrew mind loved expressing the same things (here 'I') poetically in different, parallel ways.

We can do a disservice to the authors of the Bible if we expect their words to answer questions they did not ask. The Bible uses a variety of concepts for describing people, including body, mind, spirit, soul, heart, bones and strength, and even deep gut feelings (e.g. Matthew 20:34).

We can do a disservice to the authors of the Bible if we expect their words to answer questions they did not ask.

Today, these words are translated in ways that reflect our current ideas about the coherence of the human person. So, for example, the words of Genesis 2:7 in the King James Version, 'and man became a living soul', are rendered 'and man became a living being' in most recent translations. The Hebrew word *nephesh* (soul) was not intended to depict some modern neurological aspect of a person. Instead it broadly signifies a creature that breathes, being descriptive of both animals (e.g. Genesis 1:21) and people. The important point to the authors was that God was the source of life – he 'animated' mankind by his breath (Genesis 2:7), and because of his will they became living 'souls' (c.f. Genesis 6:17). Since all our character springs from the life God gives, the word *nephesh* was also used to mean the seat of emotions (Job 3:20) and appetites (Deuteronomy 12:20).

To the Hebrew mind, therefore, the soul meant a living being, one animated by God's breath of life. Without it there would be only a dead body. What happened after death remained rather shadowy until late in the Old Testament period (e.g. Daniel 12:2). By contrast, Greek philosophers divided the body and the soul. Plato, around 380 BC, held that the soul endured after death, being unlike the body. Aristotle, his pupil, later challenged this. For him the soul (Greek word *psuchē*) meant the 'form' or pattern of the body. How the body functioned was a result of the soul's direction. However, Aristotle did suggest that the intellect might somehow be immortal.

For the Christian, only God can bestow immortality. Although in the New Testament there are a variety of usages for the words 'soul' and 'spirit', the latter word is used more as a description of someone in their relationship to God. However, the idea of the immortal soul persisted into the Middle Ages and was reinforced by Thomas Aquinas, who took up Aristotle's idea, suggesting that higher 'faculties' were immortal (although he considered that the 'baser' parts of the soul, such as the physical senses, were perishable).

In the seventeenth century René Descartes returned to Plato's ideas. His sceptical approach led him to suggest that the only thing of which he could be certain was that he existed because he could think such things. He later summarised this proposition[31] in the famous words *cogito ergo sum*, 'I think therefore I am'. The corollary was that God created two substances, thinking things and material things, which make up the whole of reality. In making this dual categorisation Descartes realised that there was a close union between mind and body, but he was unable to analyse it any further. However, Cartesian dualism rooted itself in the world. It led to a false distinction between two separate worlds of mind and material. This has posed a problem for both science and faith ever since. Gilbert Ryle caricatured this human amalgam of mind and matter as 'a ghost in a machine'.

Cartesian dualism rooted itself in the world. It led to a false distinction between two separate worlds of mind and material.

The Bible, though, pictures an individual as a unity. It uses many terms interchangeably to describe a person precisely because such descriptions are not tenets of faith.[32] The Bible is more concerned with practical aspects of the world rather than with philosophical aspects. It does not assume a mind/body split: we *are* souls rather than *have* them; we are physical beings, not possessors of physical bodies. We do not need to invoke an immortal soul to satisfy ourselves that we are made in the image of God.

> The Bible does not assume a mind/body split: we *are* souls rather than *have* them.

Recently, brain scanners (which indicate which parts of the brain are working when responses occur) have given us a clearer understanding of the integrated unitary functioning of our minds, similar to the biblical picture. The idea of some physical link existing between material and immaterial is mistaken (Descartes thought that the link was in the pineal gland). Scanners show that when we think of an idea or are aware of something, specific nerve cells in certain areas of the brain are activated. A person is a psychosomatic unity – mental thoughts and the firing of brain cells cannot be separated into two realities.

> A person is a psychosomatic unity – mental thoughts and the firing of brain cells cannot be separated into two realities.

We should not be afraid of speaking of the soul though, as its value is in resisting reductive views of humanity. But it is not some entity beyond the material body, nor only an artefact of the material body. It does not cause our responses, but neither is it just the sum of our responses (see Questions 31 and 34).

Science has led us back towards a more biblical and holistic view of human nature. The idea of the soul provides us with a reminder of the complex mind/body aspect of our nature that enables us to be creatures of the world, but also to glimpse the creator. The Christian hope after death does not rest on the possession of an immortal soul, but in the faith that resurrection will involve the recreation of the dynamic self that is known by God, to be an eternally living person in his presence (1 Corinthians 15:38; see Question 44).

Sum-up

● The Bible gives a very practical assessment of human character in all its complexity; it does not suggest a philosophical interpretation of it.

● We should avoid understanding human beings as composite creatures, made up of several distinct parts. A human being is not a composite 'ghost in a machine' (Gilbert Ryle).

● The concept of 'soul' helps us to recognise that we are neither only physical nor only spiritual. God alone is immortal and is the source of all life for his creation (1 Timothy 6:15–16).

28. Aren't genes the real gods in charge of our lives?

A popular modern myth is that we are at the mercy of our genetic material. All our behaviour is said to be the outworking of our genetic blueprint. It is thought that there is a <u>gene</u> for everything. Genes that are said to cause antisocial behaviour or homosexual lifestyle or even selfishness have provided emotive headlines in the media for some years. However, when we look at our nearest neighbours in the animal world, we might wish to highlight our behavioural differences. We share over 99 per cent of our genetic material with chimpanzees. Less than 1 per cent is different. Even two species of gibbon have differences of over 2 per cent between them![33]

If genes are gods that control us, then they are weak ones that need a complete supporting cast!

In fact, the idea that there are genes for certain behaviours is almost entirely false. Genes are often switched off in human cells and are activated to produce proteins only with particular environmental stimuli, and when combined with other genetic signals. If genes are gods that control us, then they are weak ones that need a complete supporting cast! Almost all our behaviour can be influenced by our conscious will and personal circumstances. St Paul reminds us correctly that in our dealings with God we have no excuse for any wrong behaviour (Romans 1:18ff).

Our characters are influenced by our genes, but at a secondary level rather than a primary one. It is this consequent biological level that is incredibly causally complex. One gene rarely causes one effect. It is the interaction of the whole person, including elements of mind, physiology, biochemistry and the environment, and not the genes alone that determines the result. Even in diseases which are known to have a clear genetic basis, there are still complex interactions. For example, a disease such as cystic fibrosis (CF – which results in the lining cells of the lung and the pancreas producing overthick mucus) occurs as the expression (the 'switching on') of a single genetic fault on chromosome 7.[34] Yet people who express the CF gene fault do not inevitably suffer badly from the disease. In fact, recent therapeutic advances with antibiotics and physiotherapy have lengthened the average life expectancy of CF sufferers into adulthood. We are not puppets on genetic strings.

We are not puppets on genetic strings.

Tests with twins have been used extensively to explore genetic influences because identical twins share the same genetic material whereas non-identical twins differ genetically. This research is often controversial because it is difficult to avoid non-independent responses to the twins' shared environment and history. Behaviour is partially inherited, but it is also affected by many other influences. A person is a complex mixture of personal, social, spiritual and physical elements. St Paul expresses this complexity for the whole person as 'spirit, soul and body' (1 Thessalonians 5:23; see Question 27).

Nevertheless, this modern insight, together with biblical discernment, has not prevented some scientists suggesting that our social and cultural world is the product of self-replicating genes themselves attempting a kind of immortality. This is the view of some proponents of sociobiology, also called evolutionary psychology. It is based on the extension of Darwinian survival of the fittest into all areas of life. In its strong form, sociobiology says that genes control behaviour, build culture and use it as a means of stabilising and ensuring their survival. (For the weaker assertion, see Question 30.) All we see is the result of our gene survival programme running inexorably. Samuel Butler once described this as 'a chicken is an egg's way of making another egg'! In 1995 a Scottish bishop suggested that our genes could force us to multiply indiscriminately. Our genes, and the <u>DNA</u> they are composed of, would be to blame then, not us! But genes are themselves only chemicals – they cannot answer to anyone, and they cannot be accused of being humanly selfish. As Richard Dawkins once correctly put it, 'DNA neither cares nor knows. DNA just is.' But it is both to distort and limit scientific enquiry to reduce human behaviour to the action of DNA, and exaggeration to say that 'we dance to its music'.[35] Genetic <u>determinists</u>' views seem to be quasi-religious extensions of science, open to the charge of denying human responsibility and avoiding the judgement of God (Hebrews 9:27).

Genetic determinists' views seem to be quasi-religious extensions of science, open to the charge of denying human responsibility and avoiding the judgement of God.

Few people accept this radical idea that genes build culture, however. Culture is richer and meant for more than just survival. It has developed in history rather than being a struggle against extinction. The durability of some Greek philosophical ideas and the Bible's insights is not so much due to their survivability as to the recognition that such ideas contain universal truths. Much of what we do would be pointless if this scientific theory were correct. For example, wars are fought for more than the excuse that a country wants its population (and hence similar genes) to survive, but for wider issues such as justice too.

Darwinism may seem to be a powerful and simple explanation for many phenomena in the biological development of species, but it is dangerous to use the same theory to reduce the humanities and social virtues to some kind of DNA after-effect. In a weaker form even sociobiology has realised that culture is not on such a tight genetic leash. We can hope that sociobiology may yet develop into a more informative and less dogmatic discipline.

If we begin again to categorise people on the basis of their genetic information, we are only a short step away from social eugenics and the nightmare of selective breeding suggested by Francis Galton (a cousin and disciple of Darwin). The horrors that happened later in Nazi Germany were the result, as Hitler decided who would be declared 'fit for survival'. This ideology denies the essential value of humanity and rejects the biblical truth that individuals are made in the image of God. Such evils still exist today in acts such as 'ethnic cleansing'.

Sum-up

- Our genes play an important but not definitive role in deciding who we are. In scientific jargon we say that the <u>genotype</u> does not rigidly determine the <u>phenotype</u>.

- Social behaviour cannot be reduced to being the outcome of gene survival, even though behaviour obviously does contain a genetic element.

- Extending Darwin's idea into human culture has led some to a denial of human values, and has resulted in an outpouring of evil in the twentieth century.

29. *Most of what we do is the result of nature or nurture, isn't it? These forces determine who we are and what drives us, and answer the question, 'Who am I?'*

'Who am I?' is a question that most people ask at various times in their lives. The daily routine of work, or the need to 'toe the company line', can be 'soul-destroying' at times. Theologian John Zizioulas has commented that the question 'Who am I?' contains within it a cry for a definition of a self that is conscious of its boundaries with the world around (the 'who'). It reflects, in the verb 'to be' (the 'am'), a desire to understand our place in the world and our hope that we are not limited by it; and it asks questions about the place of the individual (the 'I' asking the question) set against the many.

Down the ages, different philosophies and theologies have provided many different answers to this question. With the advent of science, and Darwin's theory of our evolutionary link with the animal kingdom (see Questions 23–25), scientists asked whether the animal kingdom could provide us with any clues that 'explained' complex human behaviour, and could answer the question of what a human being is. After all, we often compare our bad behaviour (rather unfairly) with that of animals.

Science works from the bottom up: its method is to apply simple theories in an attempt to explain complex phenomena. But is it possible to reduce the argument about the causes of human behaviour to a simple mixture of genes and environment, nature and nurture? The response has led to the emergence of two academic disciplines termed behaviourism and ethology. The former in its extreme form says that all animal and human behaviour results from conditioning by external forces. Ethologists, by contrast, point to aspects of animal behaviour that can only have resulted from some inbuilt 'programming', such as the honey bee's dance or the way day-old ducklings follow their mother's call and her waddle. They point to a genetic predisposition inherent in and favoured by evolution to produce these responses.

Today neither extreme is in vogue, but people are recognising that there is a complex interaction between many factors, including these two, that gives rise to a person. Indeed, individual and social behaviour in even simple animals is now recognised as correspondingly intricate. Fight and flight, feeding and reproduction describe the constraints of the animal kingdom, but do not completely specify the social structures of higher mammals.

There is a complex interaction between many factors, including nature and nurture, that gives rise to a person.

Some scientists picture the world as a hierarchy of complexity. The base level is the physical world (of physics and chemistry), living organisms come next, then organisations of living things and finally at the top is the cultural level. Levels of complexity reach human levels at which consciousness of our own self as an object leads to what scientist and theologian Arthur Peacocke calls a 'self-transcendence'. This ability to reflect on self leads in childhood to the formation of a

growing web of relationship that forms a sense of per-
sonhood. Limited choices become possible as we grow
up, such that we feel dehumanised if we are unable to
be agents of our own destinies.

In contrast to the animal world, humans alone have
aspirations that go beyond material needs. Burial rituals
point to the recognition of a dimension beyond.
Although animals may exhibit what appears to be altruistic and, rarely, deceptive behaviour (such as the black-
bird giving a warning call to others when danger is
close by, or monkeys keeping food from others), human
responses are clearly of a different order. We feel instinctively that we are not completely described as the sum
of our responses (economic, sexual, etc.), or are merely
the average of our parents' qualities. The human being
has the ability to go above and beyond such pressures,
to transcend them, and so gain a larger perspective than
mere involuntary response.

While science limits its definitions of self in relation to
other people and surroundings so they can be quanti-
fied, a Christian perspective on anthropology goes
beyond this and recognises that this self-transcendence
is real. It leads to a desire for a relationship beyond us,
with God. The gospel message is that God already
desires that, and in Christ he has taken the initiative. St
Paul summarises this as, 'God demonstrates his own
love for us in this: While we were still sinners, Christ
died for us' (Romans 5:8). In Christ, we see the example
of our true place as he is in perfect relationship with his
Father God (Luke 10:22). Through his ministry of reconciliation he offers forgiveness for each person of the
human race, in order to rebuild a relationship with him
(Romans 5:11). God's purposes for humanity are
embodied in Christ, and humanity's fragmented nature

finds its healing in him. Christians claim that the only way to properly answer the question 'Who am I?' is in terms of a relationship with the creator. The 'who' is someone welcomed back into the Father's welcoming arms (Luke 15:20); the 'am' is a person loved by God with a love that goes beyond death (John 16:27); the 'I' is a person whose individuality is valued by God, but who also finds his or her true place serving in the body of Christ (1 Corinthians 12:12–26).

Christians claim that the only way to properly answer the question 'Who am I?' is in terms of a relationship with our creator.

We therefore reject claims that genes control culture, or that culture moulds us. These elements do not provide a complete description of us. Our behaviour cannot be filed in convenient scientific pigeonholes because life is complex, interrelated and interlaced, and religious matters are an irreducible part of it. God, in the theistic religions, was always part of the equation (and cause of all) and no more able to be subsumed or jettisoned than any other part of human activity. Each part provides a response to the question 'Who am I?' Indeed it is the response to these forces that provides the springboard for looking beyond ourselves to spiritual things.

Sum-up

- Various branches of science provide insights into the constraints that are part of life.

- We should not view these descriptions, or the constraints themselves, as providing a complete portrayal of who we are. We are not bound by nature or nurture.

● Christians recognise that the answer to the enigma of human nature is found in a relationship not merely with others, but first and foremost with God.

30. Is religious belief like a virus?

Proponents of this idea suggest that religion, or specifically the notion of God, is like a virus – a genetic-like unit that is foreign to us and somehow has the ability to replicate and transfer into succeeding generations. Like the common cold it has swept over the world. The suggestion is that, like the common cold, it would be better if it were eradicated.

The reasoning that has led a few people to suggest that God could be described in such odd terms is due to the ability of science to provide simple answers. Such answers have been given in many cases to events in the world that were once considered mysterious. God is mysterious, therefore science should be able to come up with a reason for him, goes the argument. Now, it is true that science has devised simple and powerful tools for explaining happenings. For example, the reason why a rainbow exists, or a mechanism for the evolution of species over time is suggested. Both explanations describe and predict successfully many observed phenomena. But it is valid to ask how adequate scientific tools are likely to be for explaining religious behaviour, or even belief in God. To employ them in this fashion is tempting, but it is often to ignore a whole wealth of information.

Science as a discipline is dishonoured if it is used as a means to denigrate religion. But in the history of science the search for understanding has sometimes led to the

proclamation of anti-religious rhetoric thinly disguised
as scientific truth. This question is the outcome of such
an instance. The simple answer to it is, 'No, religious
belief is not like a virus.'

Science as a discipline is dishonoured if it is used as a
means to denigrate religion.

Sociobiology describes the behaviour of all living
things in Darwinian terms. Some writers adopt a weaker form of this approach[36] and suggest that elements of
culture are selected in history, just as Darwin suggested
that natural selection worked in the evolution of living
things (see Question 23). These elements, or 'memes' as
Professor Richard Dawkins calls them, would have
some degree of independence, and would 'jump' from
brain to brain in succeeding generations. Memes, then,
are to <u>DNA</u> what fleas are to dogs: they hitch along for
the ride. They are depicted as bits of culture, such as tol-
erance, modesty, ethics and hygiene. They develop as
they are subjected to a Darwinian pressure for survival.
We might also be tempted to add to the list a meme for
Darwin's theory or even sociobiology itself!

This weaker theory of sociobiology gives a status to
culture that is independent of genetic development.
Society does not become a meaningless pantomime, but
has an identity of its own linked through the generations. Religions and the idea of God are included among
other inheritable cultural units. Each religion is then
reduced to being the sum of selected characteristics that
leads to benefits for the population, and is constantly
tested through the millennia. Benefits often mean being
conservative to change, promoting stable societies.

However, conflict with new knowledge such as science in the last century has shown, according to some sociobiologists, that religions cannot adapt. Hence the memes for religious belief are due for eradication, and, they say, the sooner the better.

Yet a little consideration leads to the conclusion that as a total explanation this description of faith is inadequate. To believe that religion is passed on in such a way is to regard faith as being little more than the parrot-fashion repetition of a creed. Religions offer their followers a source of meaning, direction and sustenance in life. They are not related to gene survival fitness, but rather to fitness for survival with reference to more than mere biological functioning. <u>Genes</u> may contribute in building minds, but minds are often not selfish, even if genes are. The error is that what promotes fitness, and leads to survival, frequently takes second place when issues such as justice and truth arise in societies.

Religions are not related to gene survival fitness, but rather to fitness for survival with reference to more than mere biological functioning.

Charles Darwin himself was perplexed by altruism. It went against his ideas of natural selection. Sacrificial behaviour seemed to work against the survival of the bravest in favour of cowards! In an attempt to plug this Darwinian gap, some have pointed out that an altruistic act of saving one's relations might ensure the survival of kindred genes, and even necessitate reciprocal acts. But the point about such giving, even of one's life, is that it is done without counting the genetic cost. Other factors swamp it. Darwin's theory has been pushed beyond the limits of its explanatory power.

Religious altruism can go even further, as aid agency workers daily demonstrate. Genetic and social ties that are supposed to be absolute constraints are ignored, especially in a faith such as Christianity. For example, there are the challenging words of Jesus about the ties of relationship: 'Large crowds were travelling with Jesus, and turning to them he said: "If anyone comes to me and does not hate his father and mother, his wife and children, his brothers and sisters – yes, even his own life – he cannot be my disciple. And anyone who does not carry his cross and follow me cannot be my disciple"' (Luke 14:25–27). Faith is a lot more than Darwinian-propelled social conditioning. It both transcends and encompasses nature and nurture (Psalm 96:12; Exodus 20:12). It often goes against the flow of natural instincts and challenges the *status quo* (e.g. Luke 6:27).

As an account of religious altruism, the meme model is simply not able to describe the complexity of social or religious interaction. Minds are able do their own thing without reference to basic instincts. If culture is held on a genetic leash, then it is a long one, and not the only one. It is one constraint among many that blend together to form the rich and varied world we find today.[37]

It might be thought that the model would be better when it comes to the inevitability of death. Isn't religion about the after-life, the hope of immortality? Surely, it is suggested, the God-meme survives because of its psychological appeal of hope for the next world, one promoting a blind trust in the absence of evidence. This is a caricature of faith, though. Philosopher of religion John Bowker has pointed out that the major religions prior to Christianity had little or no belief in life after death.

They were not primarily about some divine escape route from life, but a way of engaging in it, as is Christianity. The Old Testament, for example, is very hazy indeed about life after death, but that did not stop Jews believing in God. A caricature of Christianity which claims that it is essentially 'Believe this and after you die you'll get to heaven' is a distortion of faith, because it is trying to detach religion from the real life that it is really interested in.

Sociobiology is the philosophy of the market place – what survives must be right. But without an external independent arbiter such as God, we cannot show that any concepts such as truth, or beauty, or righteousness have any right to prior common acceptance (see Question 2). They do not survive through fitness, but from the wisdom that to hold them is right. These are common values, and they find their homes in the world's major theistic religions. From a global perspective, atheistic disbelief is the virus that should be eradicated!

From a global perspective, atheistic disbelief is the virus that should be eradicated!

Genetics, then, must be seen as part of a bigger picture of complex social and political interactions, and simply as one determining factor among many. Humanity may well have the inherent ability to recognise God (or perhaps just to sense a numinous presence), but we can no more jettison the religious quest as an unwanted acquisition than we can discard our scientific curiosity that also seeks answers to humanity's great questions.

Sum-up

- Science will rarely be promoted successfully to the public by the denigration of other fields of enquiry.

- Faith is more than Darwinian-propelled social conditioning, as is culture in general. Darwinism should not be forced to provide an account of areas where it doesn't apply.

- The suggestion that God is like a virus is as inadequate as suggesting that culture is made up of inheritable bits.

MIND AND MATTER MUSINGS

Am I a machine just like my TV
or computer?

31. Can consciousness ever be explained? If so, does that dispense with the biblical belief that we are made in God's image?

Is consciousness solely a human trait? After eighteen years of keeping spaniels I might ask whether they are conscious, for I know a lot about them. For example, they have an accurate notion of time (meal-times generally); they can be trained to respond to some two dozen or so words, even when embedded in sentences; they recognise that when I am reading a book I have to pay them attention if they flop over it.[38] When they work as gundogs they appear to think without the use of language. But what is it like to be a dog – are they conscious as I sense I am conscious? Psychologist Donald MacKay asked, 'Do they have an "I story" as humans do?' So what exactly is consciousness?

The brain, of course, is the most complex of human organs. Around a third of the 100,000 of our <u>genes</u> are involved in brain building. With 100 <u>billion</u> (10^{11}) nerve cells called <u>neurons</u> and around 10^{13} probable connections between them that can also change (as the brain is 'plastic' rather than like a hardwired computer), any 'simple' theory of consciousness is likely to be potentially misleading. However, despite some philosophers' doubts it is quite a good working notion that this continuing wakeful awareness, this consciousness, is related somehow to brain activity. It would be fair to say that it develops and deepens as one grows up. The apocryphal Gospels that have the baby Jesus delivering a sermon from his crib are fantasies precisely because they ascribe to him an abstract symbolism of vocabulary (and language itself) which young children begin to acquire only at around four years of age!

With 100 billion nerve cells, any 'simple' theory of consciousness is likely to be potentially misleading.

Philosopher Blaise Pascal pictured the frailty of human beings like a reed, but he marvelled that we were thinking reeds.[39] Our minds are capable of ranging way beyond our environment. We can think abstractly and beyond the limitations of our surroundings, even dreaming up new worlds with our artistic skills that break cinema box-office records. We are not mentally contained by this material world; we are a 'little lower than the heavenly beings' (Psalm 8:5), although we are made of dust (Genesis 3:19). No wonder Descartes thought that the mind was a separate class of thing to the body.

Yet science can give us models to help us understand how the mind might enable this 'I story' to emerge. It used to be thought that certain mental functions such as calculation skills or vision or writing took place exclusively in a particular area of the brain. A study of people with damaged brains has indicated that there aren't precisely rigid functional areas, although the brain is not a homogenous undifferentiated mass either. The brain does have well-defined regions that major on balance, artistic skills or vision, for example. But sensory input is often processed in parallel through various stages of processing, which is then somehow recognised subjectively as a continuous awareness. Modern brain scanners show specific sites that are in operation during mental events, but it is unclear whether we are seeing the thinking event itself or just a response to it.[40] No single area of the brain seems to be devoted to generating consciousness, just as no specific cell appears to contain a memory – there are no 'grandmother cells' (that is, ones that contain an image of her) that are 'fired up' whenever she is seen. Yet our healthy brains produce a single 'self'.

It appears that no single area of the brain is devoted to generating consciousness, just as no specific cell seems to contain a memory.

It appears likely that being conscious of something is the result of the marshalling of neurons in collectives of brain cells. This is a response to the perception, internally or externally to the body. Arousal and response enables our minds to focus on a particular event, even though many other stimuli may be present. Yet what we perceive is a *continuous* awareness, not multiple or contiguous events. How this happens is unknown, and this has led some to suggest that something other than brain cells' electrochemical events causes it.

Of course, sophisticated thought requires sophisticated language, which is unique to us. We cannot get very far in our thinking without the language to take us there. We need the foundation of communication that is only possible in human beings. Our large brains (relative to our bulk – though size isn't everything) do give priority to areas that put together information when compared to other primates.

This does not mean that animals cannot think. At Columbia University's Primate Cognition Laboratory,

Professor Herbert Terrace has shown that rhesus monkeys are superior to other animals such as my dogs in making complex judgements based on number skills, and they may even be able to count.[41] However, the far greater ability of humans has led to the emergence of new levels of achievement. Language with the use of symbols, a spiritual awareness, and a far greater level of relationship than is possible in the rest of the animal kingdom have arisen. The 'I' story emerges and has its being within the enhanced social structures that people create.

In the Bible God reveals his name as 'I am who I am' (Exodus 3:14). It implies that God himself has this 'I story' too (see also Question 46), and that he is a personality, not a mere force. We are distinct from the rest of creation in a similar subjective way, as 'persons'. Perhaps it is in this sense that we are truly in his image and likeness (Genesis 1:26), although unlike him we are embodied creatures.

God himself has this 'I story'; perhaps it is in this sense that we are truly in his image and likeness.

However, the fact that we are conscious of something can't fully explain what consciousness is. Describing brain functioning doesn't explain consciousness, but it can specify prerequisites for its existence. This is not to suggest that consciousness is some sort of phenomenon added on to a creature. Consciousness requires information from both the past and the present. When we are ill this facet is often impaired and our world closes in on us, our consciousness is diminished or becomes virtually frozen in time. Without present sense and historical memory, consciousness is an empty vessel. In the Bible it was the social memory of each Israelite that formed and informed national consciousness (Deuteronomy 8:2), and allowed a relationship with God, who guided his people down future paths.

Consciousness, then, is embodied but not pinned down; it is personal, non-reducible and emergent (see Question 34). Science can only marvel at such a mystery, although it is a mystery that can be explored. What we can say as individuals before God is, 'I praise you because I am fearfully and wonderfully made' (Psalm 139:14).

What we can say as individuals before God is, 'I praise you because I am fearfully and wonderfully made.'

Sum-up

- Consciousness is a personalised and individual phenomenon emerging from the complex activity of our brain and dependent in its functioning on its links to the world around us and within us.

- Consciousness is not reducible to the electrochemical functioning of individual or groups of brain cells, but is dependent on them.

- While other animals have rudimentary consciousness, and can think to some limited degree, language and memory in all its richness in humans combine to produce a new unique creation. It is this personal 'self' that reflects the nature of a personal God as his image and likeness.

32. Freud said that he was a scientist, and thought that ideas of God came from our attempts to project ideas about our earthly fathers into heaven. Is that so?

After Darwin, Sigmund Freud, the father of psychotherapy, is one of the best-known names in nineteenth-century science. Was Freud a scientist, though? Freud certainly felt that his ideas and methods were scientific. In his lectures he noted that mankind had been dealt some great blows to its ego by science. One was that we are not at the centre of the universe (discovered by Copernicus – see Questions 5 and 13), and the second was the belief that we are not specially created and are instead descended from the animals (propounded by Darwin – see Question 23). Freud felt he had uncovered a third insult in that man's ego was 'not even master in his own house' (meaning the mind), but had to make do with scraps of information produced by a largely subconscious mind.

Freud's theories of personality arose from his study of dysfunctional people such as those suffering from hysteria. He discovered that traumatic experiences could be driven into inaccessible areas of the mind and repressed to avoid anxiety. They could later 'resurface' as odd and often compulsive behaviour. Also it was known that certain types of brain damage could result in people's behaviour becoming uncontrollable. The 'self' that appeared in the prim and proper behaviour of Victorian society was therefore a veneer, he thought. Underneath it lurked the unconscious 'animal' of drives and desires. Freud's models of personality developed over the years, but in all of them there was his understanding that the mind was a place of conflict. This arose between the desire for pleasure and the tendency to avoid pain. Pleasure was largely influenced by sexual drives, even in infancy, he suggested, but it was constrained by society.

Freud considered that the origin of God was the need for a father's protection in childhood. God was a substitute (an *illusion*, Freud called him)[42] to satisfy the feelings of helplessness in life as one 'matured' into adulthood. Freud supposed that God was a wish-fulfilment to satisfy a person's insecurity in the face of suffering and death.

Freud supposed that God was a wish-fulfilment to satisfy a person's insecurity in the face of suffering and death.

Freudian 'science' encountered two main objections. The first objection was noted by Freud's fellow Austrian philosopher Karl Popper, who recognised just how great the explanatory power of Freud's theories seemed to be. You can invent ways of fitting any behavioural observation into Freud's view of the world, whether it is religion or whatever. Freud's approach makes few scientifically testable predictions, which might refute his theories. The same is true, said Popper, of Marx's ideas (and even Darwin too, it's been suggested – Question 29). Such approaches are in many ways like astrology. It is easy to find confirmation, but often we do not go looking for disproof. Indeed, such theorists may look upon those who do so with considerable disdain!

The second objection (by Dutch philosopher Rümke)

is that the proposition that God is an illusion can itself be subjected to Freud's own theory of wish-fulfilment. Freud's conflict model certainly accorded with his own life as a non-practising Viennese Jew, who in 1938 fled with his family from the Nazis. The theory said more about Freud's life than about that of others. Freud's theory gratified his own desire that God should not exist.

Now it is true that many people make their gods from the image of a caring father, or a caring mother, and project that image on to God. But St Paul reminds us in Ephesians 3:15 that it is *from* God the Father (Greek – *pater*) that all the family (*patria* – perhaps better translated as 'parentage') in heaven and on earth is named. It is Freudianism in reverse, or rather Freud's ideas are topsy-turvy theology! It is more likely that we are correct in thinking that our poor attempts at fatherhood fall far short of the loving heavenly Father whom we should imitate. Wish-fulfilment is an inadequate interpretation of either the Christian or the Jewish faith. In view of God's charge to us, exemplified in the Ten Commandments, neither offers an easy road to follow (Matthew 7:13–14). In Christianity there is a cross to be carried in following Jesus Christ (Mark 8:34) which will not coincide with most people's ideas of a cosy existence.

It is likely that we are correct in thinking that our poor attempts at fatherhood fall far short of the loving heavenly Father whom we should imitate.

Some years later, disciples of Freud rebelled against his narrow readings of human behaviour. Carl Jung emphasised collective rather than individual experiences, and Alfred Adler emphasised the role of inferiority rather than sexual drive in motivating behaviour. Jung thought of religion not as an illness, but as a necessary part of health. He recognised what many findings have shown since: that religious people can be rather better adjusted and healthier than non-religious ones.

Jung thought of religion not as an illness, but as a necessary part of health.

These different approaches have provided the historical foundations for modern counselling techniques and psychotherapies that are far more sophisticated than Freud's. Background, personality, culture and upbringing all play a part in any person's life, but emphasising one over others will inevitably lead to distorted views of them (see also Question 28). Freud, however, was one of the first researchers to objectify an approach to the mind in order to study it. His reductionist models show how our minds are embodied more than we often care to think. Yet in Freud's theories, our 'selves' are reduced to being flimsy structures, precariously built upon the massive foundations of the mechanistic unconscious mind. Normal, healthy life is more robust than that; we should recall that Freud's theories were constructed from studies of disturbed souls, not sane ones. Freud's decision to put self-gratification as the motivator for all action was always a weakness. His ideas have now been largely superseded, though are still championed by some psychologists.

In the last five or so years of his life Freud retracted his idea that religion was just the result of an individual's feeling of helplessness. Instead he concentrated on considering an approach to the Jewish faith that high-lighted what he considered to be the repressive forces of religion. His last book, *Moses and Monotheism* (1939), explores this. It is written by a man still estranged from his religion, yet strangely drawn to it. It was a conflict he never escaped from.

Sum-up

● Freud saw religion as a kind of 'cultural neurosis', developed to make our helplessness tolerable.

● Wish-fulfilment can be used as a double-edged sword. We can just as readily suggest that it is a wish-fulfilment by atheists who try to show that God does *not* exist.

● To label belief in God as a wish-fulfilment is a way of extending a 'scientific' theory into an area where it is difficult to decide whether it is valid or not. In Freud's case, such ideas fail to account adequately for God's existence.

33. Nowadays we have drugs to help those who 'hear voices'. Where does that leave Christian claims that God 'speaks' to us?

We are all aware of the chemical basis of mental activity. It is important to realise that nerve cells, <u>neurons</u>, communicate with each other through electrochemical contact, and therefore chemicals can influence their action. Naturally occurring opiate-like chemicals in our brains influence our moods, and pain and pleasure are intensified or dulled by them. They work by altering the state of arousal in the brain via a complex feedback process. Hence it is not surprising that mood-enhancing drugs or imbalances in brain chemistry can cause significant effects. So we have to ask whether someone who claims to hear God's voice is deluded and experiencing mental states induced by abnormal functioning of the brain.

Neurons are not simply turned on or off like a switch, but exist in a variety of states of readiness, which can trigger a range of responses. This results in a variation of the potential for brain activity and changes in mental alertness. If we are highly aroused, expecting something to happen, then the smallest event may be necessary to trigger a response, whereas if we are dampened down by depression, even big events may provoke little reaction. Mood swings too may have impulsive or depressive consequences. More serious abnormal functioning can lead to personality disorders and a variety of other mental illnesses.

Perhaps the illness most associated with 'hearing voices' is schizophrenia. The sufferer is unable to control his or her thoughts as a normal person might. Conscious thoughts become like waking dreams or nightmares bombarding the mind. The conscious mind either is unable to sort out many distracting mental stimuli, or over-concentrates on a particular one. Normal behaviour and social integration become almost impossible. Drugs work to bring such symptoms under control either by enhancing communication between neuron groups or, through over-sensitising them, by damping down the subsequent response to stimuli.

When we consider religious phenomena we must ensure that we don't make a category mistake. Just because many schizophrenics hear voices as a symptom of their illness, it does not follow that everyone who hears voices is therefore schizophrenic or otherwise mentally ill. We should look at the *whole* person to get a clearer indication of their state of mind. What the person subsequently says and does will substantiate or refute their claims. Jesus' words in Matthew 7:16 are a sure guide: 'By their fruit you will recognise them.' The man who counselled that we love our enemy did so himself, forgiving them amid the agony of crucifixion (Luke 23:34).

Just because some people hear voices as a symptom of their illness, it does not follow that everyone who hears voices is mentally ill.

In the Bible, people who are open to God rarely hear an actual voice. More often they become aware of his message through dreams and visions (e.g. Genesis 15:1) or by intuition, or the wisdom of others (Exodus 18:14). Others become aware of God's will through reflecting on the words of Scripture, teaching us how to follow in his ways (Psalm 119:105–106). Each event like this will have a natural interpretation along with it. Whether particular experiences gain the adjective 'religious' depends on the frames of reference in which they are received, and in which they are interpreted. Religious awareness is often highly dependent upon location, circumstance and anticipation. The call of the prophet Isaiah at a time of national crisis is an example (Isaiah 6:8).

Whether particular experiences gain the adjective 'religious' depends on the frames of reference in which they are received.

Generally, we usually think that religious experience is mediated through ways that we might describe as 'supernatural'. However, Christian psychologist Fraser Watts warns against thinking that experiences are going to be perceived without reference to the world around us.[43] Religious experience, like all experiences, finds a correlation in brain activity, and some rudimentary understanding of this has recently been gained. Authenticity should not be considered as likely when natural explanations cannot be found. That is to entice a 'god of the gaps' back. If we only allow for God to speak to us on 'special occasions', then religion will automatically become marginalised.

Nevertheless, at certain critical times God's servants such as Moses (Exodus 3:4) and Jesus hear his voice (e.g. Matthew 3:17). We cannot uncover exactly what happened aside from the words of the text. Yet by examining other areas of their lives we can judge whether such unusual events might be valid. It is good scientific practice to ask whether those who say they hear God's voice really do lead lives that are worthy of praise (see Question 49). The beliefs and behaviour of those who are deluded will not generally match up to their claims.

It is good scientific practice to ask whether those who say they hear God's voice really do lead lives that are worthy of praise.

There is no doubt that drugs influence the mind, often irreversibly. One of the effects of Ecstasy (an amphetamine compound) is that long term it appears to destroy neurons that produce a chemical that helps us to focus on a particular subject. Yet if we can design drugs to influence our minds, why should not God be able to influence us? The behaviour of the mind is supple and open to all kinds of influences. We are not like robots, closed to new happenings, but are open to them (see Question 26). The laws of nature are so often seen as rules that straightjacket us, whereas in fact they are the means by which new things emerge.

Sum-up

● Like any organ the brain is influenced by many factors inside and outside the body.

● Although certain people with chemical imbalances in their brains can hear voices, we can only judge the veracity of their statements by examination of the whole person's behaviour.

● We should beware dividing off religious experience

from the rest of human experiences mediated through the senses, or we run the risk of marginalising God.

34. *Our conscious thoughts are the product of brain chemistry, so are they not merely subjective illusions?*

Recently science has turned its <u>empirical</u> gaze from the observable to the observer. But when it comes to the study of the human mind, science cannot completely investigate first-person sensations in terms of third-person observations. Philosopher John Searle has pointed out that our subjectivity is irreducible, and since we can observe only objects, science must be content with this limitation. Galileo rightly described science as being only about those things that could be measured. Concepts such as beauty, meaning and love fall outside this area, because they are beyond strict measurement. One could describe them as qualities, or *qualia*, rather than quantities.

Science cannot completely investigate first-person sensations in terms of third-person observations.

In the first half of this century, psychologists began to study minds and experience in different species. Yet by maintaining an entirely objective view, they could only arrive at a behavioural explanation of animal and human activity. Earlier experiments in which men and women were trained to record and report their thinking processes yielded results which depended on how they had been trained, and failed to open up any new insights into <u>cognitive</u> processes. They were dropped in

194

favour of a behavioural approach (see Question 29). External third-person descriptions made minds appear to be illusions, and mental states nothing more than the result of reactions to stimuli.

The desire to reduce human consciousness to a third-person framework doesn't fit well with our experience. Philosopher Thomas Nagel reminded scientists that the reality of first-person conscious thoughts needed to occupy 'as fundamental a place in any credible world view as matter, energy, space, time and numbers'.[44] Wisdom is more than just information and knowledge. We should beware accepting any scientific model that offers a truncated description of the world, omitting elements of the broader reality of which we are all aware.

For thirty years psychology was dominated by the behavioural approach. René Descartes' idea that there might be a separate world of non-measurable mental and spiritual realities was anathema, even a terror to many scientists. It was far safer to limit study to measurable objectivity, and to suggest that this is the only reality. Science did this by a general method called reductionism, and its thesis lies behind the question posed.

Reductionism has often been called 'nothing buttery'. For example, chemistry is the study of the interactions of atoms and molecules, but as these interactions are each describable in terms of laws of physics, it is suggested therefore that chemistry is *nothing but* physics (this is usually claimed by physicists but not chemists!). One is said to be reducible to the other. In the case of our minds, this approach says that their ontology (meaning the mind's essence or being) can be reduced to something else (*just* brain cells firing or instinctive responses to events). This reductive methodology leads to a denial of the existence of the very thing the scientist set out to explore! Although reductionist science is usually necessary to initiate an understanding of the physical world, it is unlikely to be sufficient to explain everything.

Reductionist science is usually necessary to initiate an understanding of the physical world, but it is unlikely to be sufficient to explain everything.

Therefore saying that we are 'just' something is unlikely to be adequate. We know that our minds produce concepts that are far richer than mere responses to stimuli. Even the theories of Darwinists are more than this, let alone artistic imagination! We do not understand how consciousness arises, but a description that says we are nothing more than the sum of a series of responses, like a thermostat in a heating system responding to its environment, is defective (see also Question 31). Good science requires theories to be modified when they don't fit all the data. Yet some scientists suggest these analogies to effectively deny the existence of our conscious life of thoughts and emotions.

During this century science has fragmented into many disciplines. <u>Metaphysical</u> statements such as those produced by reductionists are attempts at drawing universal conclusions that make their enquiries appear worthwhile. They are attempts to appropriate other fields as well as to consolidate their own. Reductionism does not have the monopoly on wisdom, be it human understanding or divine utterance.

Our minds may be described as 'personalised brains' (according to Professor Susan Greenfield), but an objective description cannot elbow out the inescapable fact of our own subjective world. Personalisation is not the same as personality. Scientists have begun to realise that this reductive method fails to account adequately for the properties of complex biological systems. New properties emerge that cannot be described in terms of the sum of their parts. Consciousness is one of them.

An objective description cannot elbow out the inescapable fact of our own subjective world.

Sum-up

- Science operates by an objective methodology that has in the past denied the existence of non-measurable qualities. Brain chemistry is a necessary but not sufficient description of the mind.

- First-person awareness is real, and as fundamental as third-person knowledge. We are more than brain cells firing, as the best of our culture testifies to.

- Reductionism provides an inadequate basis for understanding our world. Self-awareness brings an irreducible subjectivity into the world that cannot be adequately explained away by objective science.

35. Thinking is just computation. One day we will have computers as 'alive' as we are. By creating artificial life, won't we become like God?

In the eighteenth-century Age of <u>Enlightenment</u> people believed that everything could be explained by human reason. 'Dare to know' was the maxim coined by Immanuel Kant to summarise this. A tool of science such as the law of gravitation discovered by Isaac Newton was a prime example of this triumph of reason. In later years, poet A. C. Swinburne could dare to write in his 'Hymn of Man', 'glory to Man in the highest! For Man is the master of things', copying Luke 2:14. Today, many scientists still assert that everything will eventually be understood using the tools of science. In time science will debunk all mysteries, it's said, though this is itself a statement of faith. Philosopher John Searle calls it the 'heroic-age-of-science manoevre'.[45] Currently, as consciousness is increasing the subject of study, the tool that is said to explain it is the computer. If our brains are only sophisticated computers, then one day we might create thinking machines too, and be like God.

Many scientists still assert that everything will eventually be understood.

Currently, computers are usually digital machines, operating by using on/off signals. However, the brain functions analogically; its information is conveyed by variation in quantities. So does the brain function like an analogue computer, albeit a slow one? Computers store information well, but people remember badly. Are we, then, just inferior computers?

Computers generally work by arithmetic or similar procedures called <u>algorithms</u>, which transform an input into an output, a question into an answer. Computers do this every time, but humans rarely respond in such a strict way. What is by no means certain is that mental activities such as thought, intuition and common sense can be reduced to algorithms, a sum of instructions.

It is by no means certain that mental events can be reduced to algorithms.

Indeed, mathematics professor Sir Roger Penrose claims that insights aren't gained this way, and that even mathematical descriptions are not self-contained but rely on other rules external to the algorithms themselves (this is called Gödel's theorem – see Question 8). Mathematical insight, a small part of conscious thought, then isn't entirely computational.

Penrose noted that brains do not always think in predictable ways or follow predetermined courses. He suggests that perhaps this indeterminacy means that the indeterminate nature of quantum mechanics plays a part in generating consciousness. Other scientists propose that all details of life *can* be simulated computationally, but not exactly, because of Gödel's limitation; our thoughts are fallible and we just do the best we can.[46] Part of the problem is that we just do not understand how things like intuition, skills and talents come about. It seems likely that it is impossible to construct an exact replica of the human mind.

Minds are also not like computers in that memories are not stored in fleshly equivalents of hard disks on computers or digital videotape. Memories are subject to constant revision by our minds, often according to the feelings we had either at the time or when we recall specific events. Computer memories are identical each time we access them. Human memory is personal, and dependent on both external incidents and internal assessment.

John Searle has highlighted the difference between a computer and a person by contrasting function and intent. He calls this his Chinese Room argument. He supposes that someone (who doesn't speak Chinese) is locked in a room with a lot of Chinese symbols and is given a procedure for responding to questions given in Chinese by a person from outside. After receiving the question in Chinese, he looks up the procedural response and replies with the appropriate Chinese characters. Because the procedure is so good, the person outside thinks the man inside the room is a fluent Chinese speaker. But the man inside knew nothing of what went on (because, Searle informs us, he knows no Chinese!). He is *functioning*, but not *conscious* of the dialogue. When the IBM computer 'Deep Blue' beat world chess champion Garry Kasparov in 1997 it did not go off and celebrate, but its conscious programmers did! The awareness was not in the program, but in the programmers.

Some people think that our conscious awareness of self is at the peak of a stratification of responsive behaviour. As animals developed over time they got better at devising strategies for staying alive in a hostile world, and eventually self-awareness arose. Theologian John Puddefoot calls this awareness an inside-out world.[47] Yet that word 'eventually' represents a giant leap. We are far more than mere survival machines. We (inside ourselves) know the universe is there (outside us), but it does not know that we are. It has no conscious inside-out life.

We (inside ourselves) know the universe is there (outside us), but it does not know that we are. It has no conscious inside-out life.

Modern computer programmers in the science of Artificial Intelligence (AI) can model a few of the responses and stratagems of the mind, and even produce fun 'virtual pets'. AI tries to make machines mimic human actions and behaviour, and consequently to consider how phenomena such as consciousness, subjectivity and choice might have arisen. If computers are built that can mimic all human responses, in what respect would the computer be 'alive'? At present it is possible to build computer programs that can converse with keyboard questions from people. Yet in 1998, BBC TV's *Tomorrow's World* conducted a test (called a Turing Test) with over 1,000 conversations, trying to guess whether they were conversing with computer software or a person via an Internet link. Only around 15 per cent of people failed to spot the computer.

It is important to realise that this software was written to mimic human responses, and no doubt over the years our methods of modelling human thought patterns will improve. Currently, 'intelligent' programs for controlling the best use of a national company's service team are in production. Programs are already being written that are rudimentary learning systems. Not everything the program does is the result of direct programming.

Some things arise from within its functioning. The machine running the program can learn. In fact, in doing this programmers are following God's plan of building, in that creation makes itself (see Question 23).

AI has shown that even simple everyday tasks are actually the products of highly complex actions, and scientists realise they are many years away from creating a mind in a machine in which consciousness might arise. Currently, robotic machines reach approximately the level of a spider. The advent of computers based on information carrying large molecules (like <u>DNA</u>) will, no doubt, reach further. However, let us suppose it was done and the machine announced to us that it was a conscious being, what implications would arise?[48] First, in assessing its creators it would probably conclude that we too were persons (as each human assumes is true for others). Next it might also ask questions about purpose and meaning because, as its programmers, we doubtless would have built the capacity for general enquiry into its learning system. If we ask whether it needed to know beyond its human creator to God, then it is undeniable that having been built by those who often choose to hide from God (Genesis 3:10) it might well wish to also. Yet it would have freedom to choose. It might well choose God rather than us!

In this way we begin to see God's risk in creating beings able to be in a real relationship with him, rather than unthinking slaves. He took the risk of rejection by his people (Deuteronomy 32:20). We would create a fallible machine, in our image of fallible humanity, just as in every new generation we create fallible new life.

The mental world of consciousness we inhabit as selves seems beyond exporting into PCs, certainly at present, and perhaps ever. But if mankind does create 'artificial' life, we will not be gods, but merely show that we can do no more than we ever could do – produce life, but life with the choice either to be alienated from God's love or not.

The mental world we inhabit as selves seems beyond exporting into PCs.

Sum-up

● Information processing and mental awareness seem to be different categories of description, as John Searle's Chinese Room argument illustrates. The latter does not reduce smoothly to the former.

● We have an internal life looking out on the world, but no programming has yet produced anything capable of this.

● If we ever build a learning machine that develops an independent conscious life, it would have the freedom to choose to reject us, reflecting our freedom to either reject or turn to God.

MIRACLES OR MYTHS?

You believe that?!

36. Is this the best of all possible worlds, with all the sadness and suffering that goes on? Anyone could design a better world than God has done.

We do not have to attend the funeral of a child, say, to realise that evil and suffering exist in the world; we see it daily on our televisions. If there is truly an all-powerful, loving creator God, then the presence of evil and pain calls out for explanation. About 300 BC Greek philosopher Epicurus raised the question of why God allowed suffering. Does its presence imply that he is not able to prevent it and so is not all-powerful? If he is able to prevent it, then does that mean that he does not wish to and so is not all-loving? If he is both able and willing, then where did evil come from in the first place? Can this therefore truly be 'the best of all possible worlds'?

When Job raised the question of why he suffered, God's answer was framed in order that Job should remember that God is creator.

People in Bible times posed this double challenge to the love and power of God too, but often in a less philosophical way. They knew that turning away from God brought consequences that involved suffering (Lamentations 1:18), but they knew too of God's powers of deliverance (Micah 7:9). Yet when Job raised the question of why he suffered, God's answer was framed with reference to the whole of creation, in order that Job should remember that God is creator and ruler of all

207

(Job 38:4 and following). We could be forgiven for feeling it is an inadequate response.

Many people have suggested that the existence of pain is an insurmountable barrier to belief in a good God. Pain can certainly lead to despair and a feeling of desolation. One can deny the existence of God, or any controlling force, and say that pain is just an artefact of the natural world. Pain does warn us of trouble, it is true. It is our lot. Likewise, though, the existence of kindness and goodness makes suffering more bearable. Must they be equally shrugged off? Through the ages this attitude of resignation has not played a dominant role for the human spirit, which cries out for the answer to why suffering exists. Because we are capable of asking the question, we demand a more searching answer.

One solution given by the various world faiths is to see suffering as essentially a kind of ignorance. Hindus see suffering as the result of many existences. Suffering in one life depends on evils in a past life, and is related to attachment to worldly desires. Suffering is deserved; no God is there to be blamed. Release from reincarnation and the prison of the material world is into Brahman, an omnipresent, impersonal, non-material bliss and knowledge. The Buddhist also sees suffering as caused by ignorance of the nature of reality. Release is found in parinirvana, a state of total release from desires before extinction. The Christian witness to the Word made flesh (John 1:14) emphasises a reality other than this: heaven will be a place where sorrow and sighing will be no more, where joy in the presence of God is personally known and where material reality is not scorned (see Question 44). The new Jerusalem comes down from heaven finally as creation is renewed and God dwells with his people (Revelation 21:3).

If we believe in God and recognise the reality of suffering, then something must be done to explain the existence of evil and suffering. There are several ways that theists have done this. It can be put within God, or in opposition to God, or in the realm of the world.

Psychiatrist Carl Jung thought incorporating evil into the nature of God would solve the problem of suffering. God is then capricious, and we would do well to be wary of such a despot rather than loving him, in the same way as we might be cautious when meeting powerful but uncaring people. Everything in this view happens according to God's ordering, evil included. This solution qualifies God's goodness, and is to make him more in our likeness. Zoroastrianism follows a similar line to Jung. In contrast, Jesus' ministry of healing suggests strongly that, as he is doing his heavenly Father's will (John 5:30), suffering is not part of God's desires for the world (Psalm 30:2).

Other solutions have to qualify God's power. One suggests there is a cosmic struggle between good and evil, effectively two gods. This does little more than shift the question elsewhere. The Commandments speak of one God, not two. Also, others have suggested, if God created an imperfect world, maybe the purpose of suffering is to give us an impetus for moral struggle to achieve perfection. Such an idea of misery being for our betterment says little for those in developing countries who have little chance to get very far towards this goal. For Christians, though, some suffering can be a starting point for more positive responses (Romans 5:3–5).

If we place suffering back in the world, science has something to say. In 1710 philosopher Gottfried Leibniz began from a similar starting point to Job. He agreed that there was a good, all-powerful God. He had made the world so that the optimum for goodness could flourish. <u>Metaphysically</u>, then, the world was the best possible, but as it was finite, and therefore not God, it could not be perfect. He came to this conclusion and then saw that we cannot just wish away evil and suffering, and be left with the same kind of world. He realised that the universe had to be regarded as a whole, and all things were connected. It might appear possible to consider what a world where war didn't exist might be like, but other things would be lost in consequence, such as our freedom as autonomous creatures. God might be all-powerful, but he cannot do what is logically impossible – give creatures freedom and deny it at the same time.

Leibniz's idea of connectivity is being uncovered by science today. It shows us that in order for us to exist, the biosphere we inhabit must be as it is, dynamic and changing, and events such as earthquakes can be seen as a necessary evil (see Question 22 on conditions for life emerging). Physical evil can be justified if it occurs for a greater good, Leibniz suggested. The <u>anthropic</u> nature of our universe reveals that our habitation has been finely tuned from its inception for good (see Question 13), and is the product of a process of growing complexity and emergent awareness (see Question 31). Pleasure and pain were inevitable consequences of creating conscious beings who could freely decide to relate to God, worship him and enjoy him for ever. This is often called the free-process defence. Such are the risks any creator must necessarily take unless a world of conditioned response, of creatures with no real thoughts, is to be formed.

The existence of moral evil is often said to be the result of our free will. We have the capacity to choose. St Augustine used this as the basis of his explanation of evil's existence. All evil and suffering are the result of human sin. God created an exquisite world, but mankind's choice was to stray from him, and suffering was the result. Because sin is part of all our lives, it is not therefore undeserved. God permits suffering, and we in turn value our freedom highly.

Pleasure and pain were inevitable consequences of creating conscious beings who could freely decide to relate to God.

Science shows that throughout earth's history, creatures have always sensed pain. In the book of Genesis we are told that God saw his creation was good, but the practicality of that word for the Hebrews contrasts with the abstract way we take it. God's works are described as perfect (Deuteronomy 32:4), but this word (*ta-meem* in Hebrew) is also used of Noah (Genesis 6:9), and of those who follow God's ways (Psalm 119:1). It means rather completeness and having integrity. God in his wisdom created a world perfect for creatures like ourselves, who with intent can mess it up. Christian insight goes further and recognises that behind evil is a greater influence in the person of the devil, again allowed by God in the limited autonomy of creation. Jesus spoke of his reality and involvement in evil and suffering. The power of evil is certainly such that the biblical teaching rings true.

Such reasons may still be considered insufficient to get God off the hook. But Christians believe that God is no stranger to pain either. He is not deaf to the needs of the world. Rather, he came to this world as one of us, in the person of Christ, experiencing both suffering and rejection. His life ended in one of the most painful ways known. The cross proclaims that God does care enough to show his love in the midst of pain and suffering, using it to overcome the power of evil through the resurrection (see Question 41).

The cross proclaims that God does care enough to show his love in the midst of pain and suffering.

The Christian gospel is that God has not abandoned us to an impersonal universe. There is a theological theory that God 'makes way' for the universe – like some craftsman letting an apprentice produce his first piece of work. This is a continuing allowance by the truly loving nature of God to permit the world and mankind to blossom. But this is only for a time so that we may freely turn to him.

No heaven may be able to rectify an Auschwitz,[49] but the good of the world will not be lost for ever, but redeemed through the cross of Christ. In taking responsibility for evil, Christ dealt with it, not as an intellectual problem, but practically. Christians wait for a new heaven and earth where suffering is no more, where the necessary and contingent evil of this world is no more, and those who choose God will inherit eternal life with him. Any answer to the question of suffering must never be glib, but it can permit us to have hope. If our universe is the optimum (for we have no comparison) for freely seeking God, then the answer to this mystery will ultimately be found with him.

Sum-up

● The presence of suffering challenges the concept of an all-powerful loving creator.

- In a dynamic and interrelated universe God did not wish evil to exist, for it was not part of his plan, but he permitted it to allow real freedom to his creatures.

- The cost of creating autonomous beings who suffer is one that God did not ignore but came to share in and overcome for us.

37. Miracles don't happen today, do they? Surely they were just the products of the minds of superstitious people in the past.

Miracles form a major area of contention between science and religion today. As science has progressed, miracles begin to look less and less likely. Some theologians have aided and abetted this retreat into the safe havens of the emotions and the mystical. Miracles, by definition, occur infrequently. They are 'events to wonder at'; the Latin word *mirare*, from which the word 'miracle' derives, means just that. Science, by contrast, usually tries to explain frequent events, such as why the sky is blue or why the earth revolves around the sun as it does. So where exactly do miracles fit in?

Christianity and some other religions see the regular world as a reflection of the faithfulness of a life-sustaining God.

We live in an ordered world. In fact, the lack of a consistent backdrop to life would make it intolerable. Because of that, Christianity and some other religions see the regular world as a reflection of the faithfulness of a life-sustaining God. Genesis 8:22 echoes this when it says: 'As long as the earth endures, seedtime and harvest, cold and heat, summer and winter, day and night will never cease.' So does the psalmist in Psalm 104:14: 'He makes grass grow for the cattle, and plants for man to cultivate – bringing forth food from the

214

earth.' The constancy of God's care ensures it does, and this 'special' universe reflects that (see Question 13).

In the eighteenth century, philosopher David Hume was a major contributor to the popular notion that miracles do not happen. Science was beginning to flourish and it tightened its grip on describing reality. Hume's attack went something like this: Experience and the laws we find depend on evidence, and a wise man will fit his belief to the evidence. Repeatable experiments with the same outcome will lead us to ascertain regular laws, and deviations from these laws must be considered suspect. Laws of nature are firm and fixed, and since miracles are a violation of the laws of nature which cannot by definition be altered, therefore miracles cannot occur.[50]

Now if scientists had delved completely into the laws of nature and had a complete catalogue of them, then they might dare to suggest this. But they do not have such a list, and certainly they had a lot less understanding in Hume's day. Hume's argument is based on false premises. It takes the concept of an experiment done under carefully controlled and repeatable conditions and transfers it to the real world in which miracles are found. Hume declares, for example, that dead men normally do not rise. The overwhelming evidence is that they don't. Therefore, he declares, we can make a binding law that says they can't. Hence any miracle must be discounted because the world works only by laws. You can also always suggest reasons why any miracle might be discounted, such as unreliable witnesses or superstition. Miracles are therefore the lonings of unstable minds which wise people can now discount.

The error is that he replaces the probable with an absolute. We know that experimental science does not prove the laws it determines; it produces theories that are likely to varying degrees (see Question 2). In fact much good science has arisen from violations of laws that seemed almost certain. These violations allowed new deeper laws to be found, as was the case for <u>relativity</u>. Experience gained in the laboratory or outside it must not be used to dismiss evidence that we happen not to like. Those who declare that miracles cannot happen by definition are like Hume selecting out beforehand the evidence they do not want. This is bad science. We may not know what to do with the evidence, and it must be open to scrutiny, but we should not merely consign it to the dustbin just because it is anomalous to our preconceived ideas.

Those who declare that miracles cannot happen by definition are selecting out beforehand the evidence they do not want. This is bad science.

In response to Hume, some theologians felt constrained to abandon belief in the miraculous in the face of what seemed to be a cut-and-dried mechanistic world (see Question 26), leaving no place for God's action (or ours!). Theologian Friedrich Schleiermacher thought a miracle could only ever be the religious word for an event. Any event such as a sunset, for example, could be interpreted personally as religiously significant. In order to retain a belief in God, he was seen as a constitutional monarch who rubber-stamps a complete uniformity to nature, but little else. Many people today are quite happy with such a nebulous picture of God.

But such a view is not sufficient to explain the biblical witness of God.

The Bible speaks of God being known through his mighty deeds and acts (Deuteronomy 3:24). God does not work according to uniformity but according to his will, just as we do. St John's Gospel calls miracles *signs*, for they point to God's nature and his wishes for the world. We should not then perceive miracles as representing a change in the way God works. He works in a way that communicates his love, and in a way that elicits faith and response. It is a way that is seen in the faithful regularities of nature that we take for granted every day.

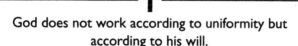

God does not work according to uniformity but according to his will.

Yet God also acts in the world, but he does this not in a way that is interventionist (as Hume assumed). God does not so much interrupt world events; rather he interacts with creation and sustains it – the history of the Israelites from the Exodus onwards being an example. Schleiermacher was only partly correct. Each event will have a religious and a natural description. A beautiful sunrise on one day, for example, may uplift someone bereaved. An ill person prayed for who recovers may thank God (see Question 39). Both occurrences have natural explanations in terms science can explore, but faith seeks an answer in terms of God's action too. An atheist is unlikely to seek this dimension. No doubt at best he would put it down to coincidence when such events happen! Compulsion is not a suitable prelude to belief in God. He wishes that it should be born out of love.

God does not so much interrupt world events;
rather he interacts with creation and sustains it.

The correct response to an extreme sceptic is not an uncritical acceptance of all things weird. Accepting that miracles may occur is not giving *carte blanche* to everything that is called 'the paranormal' today. Neither should we argue that God may do whatever he wants, including suspending the laws of nature, because we may find ourselves defending a capricious god by asserting that God caused one particular event and not another.

Some modern scientists have stepped away from an avowedly atheistic position and realised that there has been undue haste in dismissing the evidence for the miraculous and God's action in his world. In July 1984, fourteen top scientists wrote to *The Times* about their belief that science didn't eliminate miracles. Fierce opposition from latter-day David Humes ensued. There is no doubt that miracles will continue as a hot topic of debate, but scientists need to realise that defining away what is unwelcome is unscientific. The wisdom of our ancestors was often in being open to the possibility that God's world might surprise us.

Sum-up

● The regularity of the world reflects God's faithfulness as much as the miraculous does.

● Hume dismissed evidence he did not care for. Laws became prescriptive rather than descriptive, and so miracles could be discounted in this prejudiced view.

● Often what is found as abnormal in science can be a window into deeper understanding.

● God's action in the world should be seen more properly as interaction rather than intervention.

38. Weren't the miracles of healing that the Bible describes dealing with what we call psychosomatic illness today?

Nearly three-quarters of British people say they believe in God. Yet many people are not willing to ask what God can do for them, and do not expect him to give them good things. Often, scientists who believe in God over-emphasise God's faithfulness in upholding the laws of nature to the detriment of other aspects of his character. They are more concerned with religion being compatible with current scientific understanding than with challenging those who lack faith. A god who is our 'ground of being' is intellectually interesting, but unlikely to be the basis to live by, or to ask for healing from. This is not so for the God of the Bible.

God's character is far more than being drearily faithful. A husband who was faithful to his wife yet never showed her any affection would be a poor husband, because love, justice and tenderness are important emotions in any relationship. The Bible explores the relationship of the God of Israel with his people. This is the proper context in which to ask questions about miracles, not just about whether they can occur (see Question 37). Miracles occur because they tell us something of the nature and purposes of God, and his relationship with us. They are not stand-alone magic tricks, but they serve a purpose – that of pointing humanity to God. Believing in miracles for a Christian is to open the door to discovering the good intents of God.

Miracles occur because they tell us something of the nature and purposes of God. They are not stand-alone magic tricks.

Although many people do believe in miracles, some consider the miracle to be merely in the mind of the person involved rather than from God. It is suggested that miracles are the result of the powerful control the mind has over the body. Although we have no direct medical information about biblical miracles, a few of Jesus' exorcisms seem at first sight to relate to personality disorders (Mark 5:9) or epilepsy (Mark 9:20). Others, such as paralysis, might be seen as having a psychosomatic component (John 5:8).

A popular view is that anything psychosomatic is not genuine. But the mind and brain both clearly influence, and are influenced by, other organs and sensations, and science is beginning to take a holistic approach to mind/body problems today (see Question 33). Illness affects the whole person, and although often a disease is specific to one area of the body, it requires whole person treatment. Modern nursing reflects this discovery. The division of medicine into many specialist disciplines has led in the past to a piecemeal and inadequate approach that is now beginning to be rectified.

Psychosomatic components in illnesses are well known. Recently, the field of behavioural medicine has begun to study how illnesses are aggravated, or even caused, by social conditions or negative emotional states. High blood pressure and obesity have been studied in particular. A placebo *can* be effective (this is where the patient believes the 'medicine' will work, even though there are no active chemical agents present to effect a cure). One theory is that healing in a patient expecting a cure is promoted by the brain releasing morphine-like chemicals called endorphins, a class of the body's naturally occurring opiates. In fact new medicines have to show their worth in comparison with placebos in trials. Nobody underrates the power of the mind, even if its action is not wholly understood. What this suggests is that an illness and its healing are still 'real', even if the illness has a large psychosomatic component.

Modern studies suggest that an illness and its healing are 'real', even if the illness has a large psychosomatic component.

We should be wary, then, of writing off healings that can be dismissed as 'all in the mind'. Those who sought Jesus came expecting a healer. Some of these undoubtedly had psychosomatic components to their infirmities, but that does not make their illnesses any less real nor the healings false. But when crowds came, they came not only to find healing, but also to hear his message (Luke 5:15).

Having said that, there are miracles in the Bible that go well beyond these 'psychosomatic' realms, of course. God relates to all his creation, and not just to people's minds! The most important miracle is the resurrection (see Question 41), but others such as walking on water, changing water into wine, and multiplying loaves and fishes are among more 'unusual' ones. They cannot readily be removed to give a 'reasonable religion' which some have advocated. But can we get some idea as to why such strange events are occurring?

God's purposes are disclosed at particular times. The prophets testify to that. But if God acts in a way consistent with his nature, and if Jesus is who he claims to be, then there is less reason why he and his followers should be constrained within ordinary, everyday events. One of the qualities of what people call 'the paranormal' is that everything is spooky, bizarre and arbitrary; Christian witness is of a God who is not at all like that (Exodus 34:67). The events of the New Testament times aren't ordinary, because the gospel message is not ordinary. It is extraordinary. God is telling his people he is doing something new in these times. In the New Testament, miracles are done in the context of teaching. But there is a point and a logic behind what happens. For example, Jesus declares that he is the resurrection and the life, and then raises Lazarus from the dead (John 11). Time and again the miracle illustrates the message.

✝

In the New Testament there is a point and a logic behind what happens. Time and again the miracle illustrates the message.

Often some theologians have assumed that the message preceded the miracle, which was then invented as an illustration. Yet Peter goes out of his way to remind his readers that Christianity was not based on 'cleverly invented stories' (2 Peter 1:16). For example, the miracle of Cana in Galilee (turning water into wine, John 2:1–11) might pale in comparison with the level of sickness in the world. Yet it is appropriate in the context of the God who invites his creatures to a final heavenly banquet

(Matthew 22), where all sorrow and tears are no more. The biblical word for 'heal' means far more than to get physically better. It describes a complete salvation, healing, wholeness and reconciliation with God. Its scope is far greater than what we term 'recovering from illness'. It describes what the people of the day expected of the Messiah; they expected God to vindicate his people. It was the literal meaning of Jesus' name – 'God to the rescue'.

✝

The biblical word for 'heal' means far more than to get physically better. It describes a complete salvation, healing, wholeness and reconciliation with God.

If we see miracles as just a scenario for putting right human ills, our perspective will be too low; in Jesus' day many people just wanted him to eject the Roman invaders (John 6:15). Miraculous signs are not magic tricks, but point to a new reality, a resurrection hope. What else should we expect from the creator of all things? He has a purpose and a will for creation that makes the Bible not a book of incantations, but a commentary and guide of how to relate to him. A miracle should be the beginning of a person's salvation, not the end of it.

There is, of course, no reason why scientists should not study miracles. Any event should be open to both scientific and religious investigation, even if their approaches limit what they each conclude. Just as they have no place in this world, fraudulent claims have no place in God's kingdom. The Roman Catholic Church, which carefully examines alleged miracles, is correct to be wary of accepting them, and other churches should be too. But if miracles changed the lives of many men and women in Jesus' time, there is no reason why God should not perform them today.

Sum-up

● It is important to see that even psychosomatic components of illness need real healing.

● Miracles are not just in the realm of the psychosomatic. God wishes to relate to all his creation, not just to people's physical complaints.

● At times in history God may act in a way that reveals something of his purposes. Such times might reasonably contain events other than ordinary, everyday happenings.

● By believing in miracles Christians are not giving licence to the paranormal. God is logical in what he does, not capricious. Miracles should be open to investigation, whether religious or scientific.

39. Aren't answers to prayer merely coincidences that believers assign to God?

Jesus told his followers to pray – 'Ask and it will be given to you' (Matthew 7:7). The various words used in the Bible for praying all have some sense of petition. They imply that God deals with his world on a personal level (Luke 12:7). The Bible asserts over twenty times that God hears the prayers of his people (e.g. Psalm 4:1).

✝

Jesus told his followers to pray – 'Ask and it will be given to you.'

Of course, Christians also say that God already knows their needs. Praying therefore is partly a means of opening our hearts to God, of acknowledging our need for God's assistance, and of seeking his will for us. Prayer begins a dialogue with God that unpacks our motives, desires and even sometimes our prejudices and fury (Psalm 137:9). Prayer is part of a dynamic relationship with God, of abiding in him (John 15:7) but not being overwhelmed by him.

Christians have to take into account God's perspective, and so prayer is not about their wish-fulfilment. God does not need our co-operation and our commitment to do anything, but in a relationship of love he will often respond when we call to him. Prayer is not about seeing results only when our wills correspond exactly to God's, but it is the outcome of a conversation (for example, Abraham's prayers in Genesis 18:22ff.).

A scientist might validly ask: 'Yes, but does it make any difference?' Two thousand years of practice strongly suggests that it does. A sceptical scientist would want more evidence, and in fact many studies on the efficacy of prayer have been done. They generally find that prayer does indeed seem to promote health and positive attitudes to living. However, other pastimes do so too, without reference to God. But that is not the primary purpose of prayer – it is a by-product. It might help relaxation, and especially aid recovery in times of illness (see Question 38),[51] but more importantly, through communication with God, prayer gives meaning and direction to existence, despite the ups and downs of life.

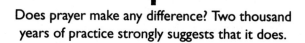

Does prayer make any difference? Two thousand years of practice strongly suggests that it does.

In the Bible, prayer also leads to deliverance from difficult or dangerous situations on occasions where that is God's will (Nehemiah 9:28). Could an experiment be done to confirm that prayer to God made a real difference? Christians may cite verses about not testing God (e.g. Matthew 4:7), yet a believer will often assess the outcome of prayer at a later date and give thanks for what has happened.[52] In 1988 the effects of intercessory prayer were examined in a way a scientist would like. A medical researcher asked for Christian church groups to pray for around half of about 400 patients in a coronary care unit. The other half were not prayed for, but the experiment was done *double-blind*; that is, neither the researcher nor those praying knew which patients were being prayed for and neither did the patients (an independent third party managed the experiment, keeping the database). The results showed that those prayed for had significantly fewer follow-on heart problems and required less subsequent medication.[53]

Although further experiments might need to be done, it does appear on the surface that 'the prayer of a righteous person is powerful and effective' (James 5:16). This might be nothing new for a Christian, but for a scientist it is evidence that does not appear to have an immediate secular solution, assuming the selection of patients was arbitrary, which it appears to have been.

Such tests don't degrade prayer in this instance. The people who prayed for the patients were as earnest as any Christians; they had active prayer lives and were part of thriving Christian fellowships. A sceptic would still be open to say the result was just a statistical anomaly, a coincidence, if maybe feeling a little uneasy at the same time. The tests do not point to how God works, but they are suggestive that he does to someone who is unsure. In a world where all events could be predicted infallibly there would be no need for prayer and no room for manoeuvre. But such a world does not exist, as the insights of chaos theory have shown us (see Question 26). The real world behaves in ways that are often not predictable, even though the laws that govern them might be. Reality is not as simple as the experiments to which science has often been limited in the past. Our freedom and God's freedom are not ruled out (see also Question 45).

Such responses of doubt are always open to mankind. God does not compel faith or it would not be faith. But as a former Archbishop of Canterbury, William Temple, once said, 'When I pray coincidences happen; when I don't, they don't.'

Archbishop of Canterbury, William Temple, once said, 'When I pray coincidences happen; when I don't, they don't.'

Sum-up

- In prayer we communicate with God with all the richness and complexity of relationship that human interaction provides.

- Scientific studies have shown the benefits of prayer, but it is not a means to get what we can; that is, it is not wish-fulfilment.

- Because prayer does work, it implies that God is interested in people as well as the generalities of the universe. Although we may get no clue as to how God works, the analogy of our own personal freedom is helpful in believing that God's freedom to answer such prayers is equally real.

40. *The virgin birth is just a myth. Such things are scientifically impossible. In his Gospel, Matthew misapplied an old prophecy. If he was mistaken at such an important point in Jesus' life, how can I trust the rest of his Gospel?*

Like every faithful Jewish person, St Matthew believed that the Old Testament spoke of God's promises to his people. In it there were prophecies that spoke of deliverance from all kinds of evil. For example, Isaiah once gave a prophecy to doubting King Ahaz: 'Therefore the Lord himself will give you a sign: The virgin will be with child and will give birth to a son, and will call him Immanuel [which means God with us]' (Isaiah 7:14). Over 700 years later Matthew relates this prophecy to Jesus (Matthew 1:23). Taken out of context, his usage looks bizarre to the modern mind. In the context of Isaiah's day the prophecy related to a demonstration by God that overbearing neighbouring countries would be laid waste before the child in question was weaned.

The child that Isaiah talks of seems to mean his son, possibly with a new wife. The Hebrew word (*'almah*), often translated 'virgin', is used elsewhere of Rebekah (whom Isaac married, Genesis 24:43). Unmarried young women were almost always virgins in those days (the Greek translation uses the normal Greek word *parthenos* for virgin[54] since the rabbis knew this too). Yet Isaiah's son seems to be normally conceived and born (Isaiah 8:3).[55] But in this event Isaiah signals that they would see God as Israel's redeemer. St Matthew, then, is not using the ancient scriptures to make up new stories after the event, but he is looking back at his heritage, and explor-

ing something of what had happened in the coming of
Jesus.

✝

St Matthew is looking back at his heritage, and
exploring something of what had happened in the
coming of Jesus.

Part of the answer to the usage is given by Matthew
himself when he says that this took place to fulfil what
the prophet said (Matthew 1:22). The word 'fulfil'
means to complete or fill up full. Now Matthew realises that Jesus is the *ultimate* demonstration that the
prophecy was at last *full*-filled. Equally when he uses
a passage from Hosea 11:1, 'Out of Egypt I called
my son' (Matthew 2:15), meaning Israel in Hosea,
Matthew recognises that in Jesus ultimate redemption
from sinful slavery can occur. What has a meaning in
one event (the Exodus) widens to encompass slavery
to sin in every person's life, dealt with by Christ on
the cross.

✝

Matthew realises that Jesus is the *ultimate*
demonstration that the prophecy was at last
full-filled.

Sometimes it is asserted that other religions in biblical
times also claimed such births. However, the descriptions are often taken from accounts that are clearly
meant as stories in their entirety. In the gospel accounts
this is far from the case. We should remember as well
that the Jewish people were always very reluctant to
add pagan ideas to their faith. Yet in Jesus these

Jewish disciples experienced someone who rocked their idea of what God would do.

The virgin birth (properly, the virginal conception) is peripheral to Jesus' ministry and the church's mission in the same way that the early childhood of someone famous today might also be marginal. But why should later writers have bothered to make up something additional? Yet sprinkled throughout the New Testament documents are pointers to something unusual in his birth. Examples are Mark 6:3 (Mary's son; *not* Joseph's), Galatians 4:4 (born of a *woman*, which in a patriarchal society was an unusual comment to say the least), and possibly also Revelation 12:5 and John 8:41b. This implies that this one event is not part of some later colourful legend ill-fitting with the account of Jesus' ministry. Matthew and Luke (a doctor!) are both quite clear that a virginal conception took place (Matthew 1:23; Luke 1:34), and that it is another strand of God accomplishing his will.

Many people today doubt the virgin birth because they think that it cannot happen *a priori* (see Question 37). Such a conclusion, though, is poor science. It is scientifically true that a birth without male sperm, which supplies the Y (male) chromosome, can't obviously at first sight produce a male child. Yet in 1993, Sam Berry, Professor of Genetics at University College, London suggested several routes by which it could occur, though it would be highly unusual.[56] He was not so much supplying possible mechanisms from which a virginal birth might occur, but attempting to show that modern science cannot claim that virginal conceptions can *never* happen.[57] Matthew and Luke cannot be dismissed as superstitious story-tellers, leading us to mistrust their Gospels.

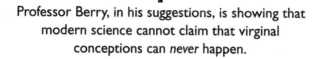

Professor Berry, in his suggestions, is showing that
modern science cannot claim that virginal
conceptions can *never* happen.

We cannot prove the virgin birth occurred, but the
witness of the early church is strongly that it did happen. Luke reminds us that this task is performed by the
power of the Holy Spirit (Luke 1:35). According to
Scripture, the life of Jesus was unique, and his followers
recognised that through his ministry he provided the
means of salvation for all. But that life which saw God
at work required a starting point in a womb. The
accounts show how God took that initiative in the life of
Jesus of Nazareth from before its earliest moments.

The accounts show how God took that initiative in
the life of Jesus of Nazareth from before its earliest
moments.

In this birth, the prayerful hope of Isaiah that God
would be with them was fulfilled in the statement that
Jesus was born of Mary. Matthew recorded what he
knew to be true, but he could not begin to understand it
aside from scriptural testimony, and we can do little
more. For the miracle is not so much the virginal conception as the Incarnation – that God came to be with us
in order to rescue us. This is the prologue to the virgin
birth. The challenge of the Incarnation is to question our
notion of space and time (see also Question 45). Older
views of space and time make this difficult. The Greek

philosopher Aristotle thought of space as a receptacle. Newton followed these ideas by conceiving of God as the container itself. With such a rigid and absolute view of space and time, it is impossible to think of the Incarnation in any way except as some kind of intervention by God (this did not trouble Newton, as he did not believe in the Trinity anyway).

Such thinking has pervaded thought even up to today. However, Einstein's theories of <u>relativity</u> dash all concepts of an absolute space and time, and replace them with relational dimensions. This is how the early church saw the power of God as well. It is God's relationship with the world that keeps it in being; it was made through Christ and has its existence through the sustaining power of God. There was no separation between our notions of the spiritual and the physical world. In the Incarnation, God identified with and acted in the world in a manner that uniquely shared our condition.

The early church sought to do justice to the person of Christ and divine participation in space and time. Here they saw the commitment of God to creation. Belief is a matter of commitment that in Jesus divine and human have come together in a way that has both a continuity with old humanity, and also gives us the hope of eternal fellowship with God (Hebrews 2:17–18; see also Question 46). Matthew and Luke are not therefore misusing prophecy, but recognising that God in Christ has taken a new initiative, and one that is according to his promises (2 Corinthians 1:20).

Sum-up

● Old Testament prophecies told about God's action in

the world. In the person of Jesus his followers realised that God was somehow with them.

● Matthew tries to convey this initiative by God in a way that his listeners will understand. It begins with the very earliest point of Jesus' life on this earth, and it states that in the virginal conception God was incarnate. The doctrine of the virgin birth conveys this mysterious truth.

● Science does not shut the door completely on the possibility of the virgin birth. Therefore we should not lightly dismiss the rest of the message of the gospel writers.

41. How can a rational person believe in the resurrection of Jesus?

Before considering whether Jesus rose from the dead, a scientist might validly ask whether Jesus really did die on the cross. After all, if he did not, that would stop any discussion about a possible resurrection, and turn it simply into a debate about recuperation! However, the Bible witnesses tell us that he certainly did die. The observation of the separation of blood and serum after death recorded in John 19:34 is scientific testimony to that. In addition, the Romans were experts at crucifixion. There was no way a centurion would allow someone who had merely swooned to be taken away to recuperate, or the soldier himself would have been there in his place the following day! Neither were they foolish enough to crucify the wrong person as has been proposed. Roman soldiers were very thorough and professional at killing. Jesus really died.

Before we conclude that Jesus came back to life by a miracle, it is reasonable to ask also whether the disciples could have engineered the belief either through wish-fulfilment, or subterfuge or mass hallucination. Several arguments point away from this.

First, the Jews had no agreed doctrines about what happened after death. There was a whole spectrum of understanding, but belief in God didn't automatically carry with it any significant belief about life after death. The psalmist in the Old Testament cried, 'What gain is there in my destruction, in my going down into the pit?

Will the dust praise you? Will it proclaim your faithfulness?' (Psalm 30:9). Perhaps at best someone might be remembered by his offspring (Proverbs 10:7). The Sadducees, Jews who were politically content with the status quo, did not believe in resurrection. They would agree with George Bernard Shaw in saying, 'I believe that when I die I rot!' Even some Greek philosophers who had so much to say about the separation of body and soul don't seem to have made much of an impact on the commonly accepted idea of the finality of death. A very prevalent tomb epitaph from those times was 'Take courage, no one is immortal'!

Belief in God didn't automatically carry with it any significant belief about life after death before the time of Jesus.

Opposing these ideas were parties such as the Pharisees, who looked for a release from the yoke of the invading pagan Romans. Between the years of Old and New Testaments, martyrs for the independence of Israel from oppressors like the Romans had expressed the view that even though they died they would be vindicated through resurrection. This was often expressed in very physical terms, but they also borrowed from Greek hopes for a 'spiritual world'. Biblical verses like Daniel 12:2–3 or Job 19:26 could be interpreted in a way that involved a physical resurrection or a spiritual afterlife, or something in between. Such a vindication had not happened by Jesus' day. Many also believed in a messiah who would come and, as God's agent, lead the people of Israel to victory, and re-establish the rule of God and an era of righteousness for redeemed Israel. Some thought the dead would live again in new bodies upon the renewed earth.

Theologian Tom Wright points out that there was no antithesis between national and individual hope, between the political and spiritual.[58] The hope was that Israel would be truly redeemed and forgiven. Resurrection was the lot for all Israel, but in some distant hoped-for future. Martha signals this in John 11:24 when answering Jesus when she says of dead Lazarus, 'I know he will rise again in the resurrection at the last day.' First-century Jews did not expect individuals to rise from the dead on an *ad hoc* basis, but when God's redemption finally came. So when Jesus began to tell the disciples that after his death he would rise, they were bewildered. St Mark tells us: 'They kept the matter to themselves, discussing what "rising from the dead" meant' (Mark 9:10).

Secondly, Jesus' manner of death was regarded as a curse in the Hebrew scriptures (Deuteronomy 21:23), a mark of being forsaken by God. No immediate resurrection was seriously expected by the leaders of the day; even the tomb guards were a token gesture in case the disciples stole the body (Matthew 27:64). So when Jesus died on the cross, the disciples were humanly beaten. They had no reason to steal his dead body because they had no expectation of an immediate resurrection for a condemned man. Jesus had told them, but they hadn't understood what he said (Luke 24:21). Subterfuge therefore looks unlikely. Subsequent persecution revealed no hint of this either; the authorities would have been very keen to find such information (cf. Matthew 28:12–13).

Thirdly, when Jesus died, his disciples would have felt both grief and guilt. After all, they had abandoned their master (Mark 14:50), and even denied they knew him (Mark 14:71). They might wish to deny Jesus' death to themselves as a group, but such a negative belief would not form the basis of a *positive* declaration that he was alive again. If Jesus had remained dead, then the process of grieving might possibly have led them eventually to the idea that somehow his Father God in heaven had vindicated him. Yet such a natural process would have happened over many months or years, not in three days. There were many other pretend messiahs around Jesus' time who died violent deaths, yet none of their followers dreamed up a spiritual resurrection. What changed the disciples' minds was meeting their risen Lord.

Jesus' retinue consisted of down-to-earth people such as a tax collector and fishermen. The men and the women who followed him were hardly academics; neither were they romantics longing for some future Shangri-La. The Hebrew people were practical, down-to-earth folk for whom death was not somehow nothing at all. Evidence of resurrection would require an empty tomb, and they found it on Easter Day. Like some experiment that yields unexpected results, the disciples found themselves surprised and confused when the risen Jesus met them.

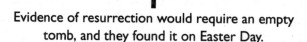

Evidence of resurrection would require an empty tomb, and they found it on Easter Day.

They later proclaimed what had happened with all the uncertainty of eyewitnesses not knowing precisely what to make of such events. They are reporting actual events rather than making up stories to persuade sceptics. The absence of a completely agreed testimony favours the truthfulness of the events, not the reverse. St

Paul himself tells us that on one occasion over 500 witnesses saw Jesus and many were still alive when he wrote (1 Corinthians 15:6). It was public knowledge, not later private conjecture.

Christians do not say that generally dead men rise, but they do say that *this* man Jesus rose, unexpectedly, but just as he predicted. The disciples went back to their Bibles and realised that there were glimpses of hope in prophecies recorded there (e.g. 1 Peter 2:24; compare Isaiah 53:4–6). Before, they had been defeated and leaderless, but now their leader was alive. They became fearless people who 'turned the world upside down' in consequence.

✝

Christians do not say that generally dead men rise,
but they do say that *this* man Jesus rose,
unexpectedly, but just as he predicted.

The role of science is to interpret surprising observations without prejudice. How should the resurrection be viewed in a scientific age? The disciples do not report that Jesus was somehow resuscitated. If they had, all we would need to say is that since all chemical reactions are reversible, Jesus might be able to live again. But this new bodily existence of Jesus was different in many ways. The risen Jesus appeared in a locked room with them (John 20:19); he showed them his nail-pierced hands and his side. He was not some sort of apparition, for he met his disciples and ate fish with them (Luke 24:42– 43). He was the same Jesus, only different. The renewed world, the kingdom of God, had already begun with the coming of the true Messiah.

The resurrection of Jesus does not fit into the notion of

a materialistic worldview, because its events take us somehow beyond this world, beyond material death. Yet a scientist must weigh the evidence no matter where it leads. In science many strange properties of matter, such as the wave/particle behaviour of matter, are beyond simple understanding in terms of the things of the world (see Question 18). Yet scientists are prepared to trust their mathematical models and recognise that however bizarre, this is what the evidence points to. This is what the disciples of Jesus had to do. They recognised that Jesus had died on the cross in our place; God was accepting the guilt of all humanity, not just Israel, in his Son. By his death Jesus gave the opportunity for all to be his people.

Science has made many ground-breaking and strange discoveries about this world. It has changed the way we view the world and our understanding of it. If this evidence is true, and the facts are themselves secure to a degree unparalleled in history, then it requires a shift in understanding over the finality of physical death. If Jesus is risen, then he is the Son of God as he said, and his teaching is true. Jesus once said to a grieving woman, 'I am the resurrection and the life. He who believes in me will live, even though he dies; and whoever lives and believes in me will never die. Do you believe this?' (John 11:25–26). Often in research a scientist may commit himself or herself to a theory in the hope that it will subsequently prove to be true. With Jesus' resurrection we need to do the same.

✝

If Jesus is risen, then he is the Son of God as he said, and his teaching is true.

One final point. The resurrection is not just another religious belief. If Jesus is alive, and the evidence is strong that he is, then you can get to know him, just as you can any living person. This is where experience comes in. Christians down the century have not just stopped with intellectual assent, but have made a personal discovery – Jesus is alive! That encounter is the start of a life-transforming and enriching experience that is offered today as then. It begins with a prayer of acceptance, and continues with a growing relationship of trust and forgiveness (see Question 50).

Sum-up

- Belief in God did not lead to recognition of an automatic belief in life after death in Old Testament times.

- When Jesus died, the disciples would have seen it as a final defeat. This rules out many of the suggestions of them engineering a 'happy ending'.

- Science has found much that goes beyond simple discernment; the resurrection is another example worthy of investigation.

- If Jesus is risen, then he is the Son of God as he said, and his teaching is true. But another world is glimpsed from this evidence too, where life with God is offered to all.

FUTURE SHOCKS
This world or the next?

42. Why does the Christian response to innovation always appear so negative? Can't we hope that technology will continue to build a perfect world?

In the twentieth century, popular support for science has grown largely because of the benefits people have derived from its technological applications. However, *technoscience*, as it's sometimes dubbed, has proved to be a double-edged sword. It has produced real threats of environmental holocaust and genetic catastrophe. Although technology has increased leisure time for some, for others it has led to redundancy. Expectations for longer lifespans from technological improvements make this even more of a strained scenario for individuals. Technology has also been the means by which smaller workforces have been made to work harder in the wake of over-zealous slimming down by companies. Consequently, the technological dreams of governments in the past have faded in the public mind, but what has been raised in its place is an ethical anxiety for the future. Such ethical concerns have seldom been the concern of those in the laboratory, interested as they are in more abstract discoveries.

Technoscience has proved to be a double-edged sword.

If we recognise that not all technological innovations are likely to be equally beneficial, then we need to agree that some ethical framework is needed for encouraging some enterprises and restricting others. Ethics are usually based on voluntarist principles today. Morality is the product of the will of humanity, both socially and individually, and increasing fragmentation of society is leading to a morality that is decided by the individual, including the scientist. For many people today one answer is found in Jeremy Bentham's *utilitarianism*. This suggests that actions are right if they produce the greatest good for the greatest number. However, increasing communication and access to all areas of the world show that such ideas have often degenerated into the exploitation of the few by the many. The universal can quickly, through self-centredness, become the egotistical.

Other people follow Immanuel Kant's ideas, which focus on motive. We do not always know what results scientific advances will yield. Concentrate on motive therefore, suggested Kant, and act as if the principle on which your action is based were to become a universal law. Treat others as an end, never as a means. Although Kant's view has echoes of the biblical injunction 'Love your neighbour as yourself' (Leviticus 19:18), a Christian ethic will look beyond personal habits and desires, and from a merely subjective position, to Christ. In the cross we see Jesus dying for others (Mark 10:45), and not saving himself.

A Christian ethic will look beyond personal habits and desires, and from a merely subjective position, to Christ.

Christian ethics must derive from the gospel of Christ. In the resurrection of Christ we see that God has reasserted his love for creation (see Question 41). The first Adam is redeemed by the second (Christ; 1 Corinthians 15:22). In the ministry of Jesus we are given a clear indication that God wishes to transform his creation, beginning with people who respond to Christ's call (2 Corinthians 3:18). A distinctively Christian response will need to avoid two pitfalls. One is a voluntarism that has no roots in human affairs, and that separates the world into the religious and the secular. Commandments then become effectively house rules for Christians who have little to say to others in dialogue. The other is an ethic that identifies with culture entirely, and which denies that the church has any moral authority to make known its views gained through revelation.[59]

Our attitude to technology, then, should be made in the light of Jesus' ministry and message, and in recognition of the Spirit of Jesus directing us. As we look at the many positive acts of Jesus, in healing, challenging and teaching us how to live, we should not be misled into thinking that the role of a Christian is only to forbid technological improvements. Rather the Christian will be at the forefront of assessing a Christ-like response.

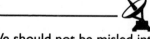

We should not be misled into thinking that the role of a Christian is only to forbid technological improvements.

The problem today is that progress in technology has become synonymous with progress in civilisation. Frequently, too little assessment of impact has been made before the technology essentially introduces itself, often at the behest of economics. If a scientist can objectify the world to study it, then an entrepreneur can also exploit it (see also Question 10). A more balanced view of what society should sanction is needed to ensure that some rein is kept on new technologies. The scientific community is not separate from the wider community but is responsible to it and through it to God.

In the case of human embryology and fertilisation, such ethical concerns are being addressed in discussion and legislation not only in Europe and the USA but worldwide. Whilst work on nuclear materials required countries to enact it, individual companies can readily research genetic issues. <u>Cloning</u> too has elicited a public debate where even proponents are recognising possible pitfalls,[60] and admitting that genetic engineering may pose real long-term risks to all life (see Questions 43 and 47). Public fears over genetically modified crops, and genetically modified organisms (GMOs) in general, have highlighted the historical reality that human controls have often not been effective enough because a more complete understanding of ecological risks has usually not been attempted.[61] The difficulty so often with technology is that it doesn't quite produce what is wanted (as Kant realised), and consequently the results restrict our freedom, often in devastating ways.

Technology will not build a better world automatically, but it can be one means of achieving it. The Christian who bases her ethics on the ministry and teaching of Jesus will take a long-term perspective that reflects God's continuing care for creation, rather than looking at short-term political ends and economic exploitation. She will take a view that seeks to remove the oppression and injustices in life, and seeks the healing between nations and within society. It means being motivated to work for a fairer sharing of resources, so that those in poverty also have the luxury of being able to contribute actively towards society rather than being the passive recipients of aid.

Technology is an inseparable part of the modern world. But it must always be a tool for the betterment of the world. It needs frameworks of ethics that give reasons for taking the next step in discovery or holding back. In history the step has so often been taken before the consequences were thought through. The horror of the scientists at the first atomic bomb test arose because they had left it to politicians to decide whether to make it, rather than help to police it themselves. Physicist Leo Szilard, who first thought up the idea of a chain reaction, attempted in vain to get the work stopped before the inevitable happened and hundreds of thousands died.

Technology alone cannot build a perfect world precisely because technology and science are human endeavours. The prophet Jeremiah knew that people's hearts were both deceitful and corrupt (Jeremiah 17:9). It is a change of heart, a new heart and a new spirit, that is needed first of all, if the goal of following God's path of life is ever to be reached (Ezekiel 11:19).

Technology alone cannot build a perfect world precisely because technology and science are human endeavours.

Sum-up

- Technoscience has been a double-edged sword in human history.

- Science and technology are done by humans and so

are subject to human failings in their implementation and development. Christian ethics need to be brought to bear in regulating innovation.

● The Bible is clear that a change of heart is needed if humanity is truly to follow God's path of life.

43. If evolution is correct, then won't we evolve into superbeings eventually, and even become divine? With genetic engineering, isn't this possibility now dawning?

In the long history of the universe, human beings have only recently appeared on the scene. At some point they could recognise themselves as 'selves' (see Questions 25 and 31). The flowering of humanity represented a fresh chapter in the history of the universe. Alfred Wallace, co-founder of the theory of natural selection (see Question 23), wrote: 'Natural selection could only have endowed savage man with a brain a little superior to that of an ape, whereas he actually possesses one very little inferior to that of a philosopher.'[62] Even primitive tribes that Wallace and Darwin described are now known to have had our mental capacity.

However, while natural selection focuses on gradual changes, the fossil records show that there have been five occasions where major extinction took place and nature appeared almost to start again. The extinction of the dinosaurs and subsequent emergence of mammals around 65 million years ago is one of them.[63] Evolution is not smooth, but interrupted with mass extinction. Evolution works on a timescale of millions of years, but extinction works in millennia.

How will the human race evolve? For most of the twentieth century the earth has been subject to the worst exploitation and ecological degradation ever. We are well able to destroy both the world and ourselves in the next millennium. We do not have the leisurely luxury of a long evolutionary timescale to become better people. It is more likely that we will destroy ourselves in what palaeontologist Richard Leakey has called *The Sixth Extinction*. On average, a species lasts about 5 million years or so; we may last much less if we are not careful. Indeed, Sir Robert May, Professor of Zoology at Oxford, has noted that this is the overall rate over 500 million years or so, yet in the last century the extinction rate suggests a species lifetime of only around 10,000 years. This is a thousand-fold increase in extinction rate. We may not have much time left!

We do not have the leisurely luxury of a long evolutionary timescale to become better people.

Natural selection is about slow adaptation to environment, but with the advances in genetic engineering we appear to be able to make rapid changes. It offers the possibility of eliminating inherited diseases and even making future generations 'to order'. Can we make 'perfect people'? Such ideas are still in the realm of science fiction, but with genetic engineering the threshold of such possibilities has been reached. How we set our scientific sails will determine the future course of this knowledge.

Today genetic engineering on human beings can be classed as therapeutic and non-therapeutic. Within these areas are changes that are made that stay with the person and are not passed on, so-called somatic therapy, and changes which affect cells that lead to sex cells for reproduction, so-called germ-line therapy. Additionally, changes to an early embryo before sufficient cell differentiation has occurred may affect all cells and consequently be passed on.

This, of course, begs many ethical questions about the status of a person, but Christians will want to lay great stress on relationship to God as creator and redeemer. This will override limited definitions of persons that highlight mental or physical health, or productivity, or ability to communicate. When we consider human beings with serious illnesses, or degenerative diseases, or the disabled, we should not devalue them as persons but see them as 'the least of [my] brothers' (Matthew 25:40). Therapeutic aspects of somatic genetic engineering represent a means of improving medical help for those in need. We should follow the example of the man who healed lepers (Matthew 11:5).

If therapeutic germ-line changes can be made that wipe out an inherited disease, such as muscular dystrophy, should they be done? Clearly the object is the elimination of a particular illness, and to allow future generations to be free of it also. Although great care is needed in assessing applications of research, future monitored trials must be supported, while recognising the danger involved in acquiring such power. However, significant progress is some way off. At present the human genome project (officially begun in 1990) is advancing towards identifying all the genes in the nucleus of a human cell. It is hoped to establish where specific genes are located on the chromosomes, and to determine, by a procedure known as sequencing, the genetic information that is encoded in the DNA. The aim is to associate specific human traits and inherited diseases, and to assist therapeutic and preventive medicine by unravelling the basic biochemical processes that cause disease.

In the case of non-therapeutic genetic manipulation, the situation is rather different. The lack of physical strength, high intelligence or even musical ability can be seen as a limitation, but how far should these things be sought? If the person is very young or still developing in the womb, how far is genetic manipulation 'making' a human being to order? Is this very different from parents who push their children to fulfil their lost ambitions? In some ways it is, for it can be seen that designing children is to go beyond begetting them, and to make them ends for our gratification (see Question 42). Such a procedure goes far beyond evolution, and towards eugenics. It is a further step down the path of consumer greed. Someone who 'wants' a child (as if it were another commodity), becomes someone who wants 'a particular type of child'. In the case of non-therapeutic somatic manipulation, ends are similarly suspect. Muscle-building by athletes using chemicals such as anabolic steroids is already seen as cheating. There is in non-therapeutic genetic engineering no final goal to be achieved and assessed, only degrees of subjective improvement.

Designing children is a further step down the path of consumer greed.

Humanity has always tried to transcend itself. The expulsion from Eden (Genesis 3:22–24), and the Tower of Babel in Genesis 11 point to futile attempts to transcend our limitations both individually and as a race. But if we are years away from bettering our lot, then the Christian message is that God has already addressed the question of how we might find a better way. The Bible talks of God's rescue of humankind from its worst enemy – itself. Like God we can know good and evil (Genesis 3:5), but we do not have the spiritual ability to choose the former rather than the latter (Romans 7:21). Our reading of human creation (see Question 25) has emphasised a development culminating in God's revelation to a creature able to respond adequately. The classic doctrine of the Fall identifies this with Adam, in the account of creation, revelation and disobedience that we all fall prey to. In Romans 5, St Paul relates the universality of sin back to Adam, from whom it has been passed down in propensity to all (Romans 5:12). Although a specific individual is in mind, he recognises a common responsibility for sin rather than just a past individual's one. The events of Genesis 1–4 should not blind us to the fact that sin and a consequent turning away from God, that leads, says St Paul, to death, needs dealing with for all humanity. He reminds us that conscience as well as law provides a basis for deliberate wrongdoing (Romans 1:32). Humanity has shown itself historically to be unable to better itself.

The Bible talks of God's rescue of humankind from its worst enemy – itself.

However, through Christ's death on the cross we are reconciled to God (2 Corinthians 5:21). St Paul recognises that we are not just delivered from sin, but to a new status and participation when he writes, '... by grace you have been saved. And God raised us up with Christ and seated us with him in the heavenly realms in Christ Jesus' (Ephesians 2:5–6). The early church fathers expressed this in such words as, 'He became man that we might be made divine.'[64] By this was not meant that we were naturally divine, or can become so through thought or deed, as in some New

Age ideas. Rather, it tells of God's sole initiative in the process of incorporating us by baptism into the divine humanity of Christ that we might become adopted children of God (John 1:12).

The eviction from Eden, where we tried to be like gods, is a commentary on behaviour where we turn from God and consequently mix up the creator and the creature, maker and made.[65] Worship turns to idolatry since we are creatures who must worship. Part of that idolatry is a self-worship that inevitably denies us becoming gods by our own hands (Romans 1:23). In our ability to do evil we are unsurpassed, and far from God (Romans 3:23). Given our history, human nature is more likely to genetically engineer devils rather than gods, as Mary Shelley chillingly explored in her novel *Frankenstein*! But even given that marred image, God thought us worth hanging on to and redeeming in order that we might dwell with him for ever (Romans 7:24 –25).

Given our history, human nature is more likely to genetically engineer devils rather than gods.

Sum-up

● Evolution has been characterised as much by rapid extinction as the slowly increasing complexity of creatures. We should not imagine we have an evolutionary timescale available to us, given our capacity for evil and destruction, as characterised this century.

● Genetic engineering is an example of the dangerous power we are gaining. We should be aware of the need for its regulation. We are more likely to design devils than gods! Therapeutic avenues are more Christ-like than non-therapeutic ones that owe more to greed than compassion.

● God did not leave us without the hope that redemption is possible for his creatures who have turned away from his offer of life since Adam.

44. One day we will be able to download our minds into machines. Isn't that immortality?

There is little hope for this universe in the long run. It will either end in perpetual cold, if gravity loses out to the Big Bang expansion (which many scientists today consider to be the most likely outcome), or it will end in burning heat as the universe is sucked back in on itself (see Question 14). In addition, this beautiful and complex cosmos is perpetually running down, and becoming increasingly disordered. Science describes this in the universal <u>Second Law of Thermodynamics</u>, which says that as time passes things tend to become less organised, because there are many more disorganised states than organised ones. This increase in disorganisation is measured by a value called <u>entropy</u> – entropy and time flow together for us. It matters not whether the universe is expanding or contracting; entropy inexorably increases. The mislaid car keys are but a foretaste of doom for all those who have hope of this world improving! Those who do have hope in that alone are to be pitied (cf. 1 Peter 1:21).

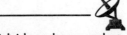

The mislaid car keys are but a foretaste of doom for all those who have hope of this world improving!

However, this bleak prognosis has not stopped some scientists from wondering if there is a material future for life itself. What might be achieved before the final curtain comes down? The lifetime of the universe as we understand it today is of the order of tens of <u>billions</u> of years. Long before our sun has died in several billion years' time we might have made great technological strides (see Question 42) and even begun to explore the stars. Perhaps, they suggest, barring many contrary indications in the twentieth century, humankind can avoid annihilating itself.

Eventually, though, matter itself will decay, and all carbon-based life forms will become extinct. But could 'thinking life' – self-aware creatures – 'convert' itself to other forms and survive? A few cosmologists think so. Part of our thinking processes might be downloaded into computers in the form of software. As our universe cools down, less energy is needed for information processing. Life would be slower 'in the cold lane', but at least it would carry on!

American cosmologist Frank Tipler has suggested that even after physical death we could be resurrected in giant, enormously powerful computing machines that utilise the energy of the galaxies.[66] This kind of resurrection would be a simulation of the past, with both good and evil replaying the tussles of previous centuries. In this way Tipler feels that life in the universe is destined never to die out, but will expand to fill it. He calls this his final <u>anthropic principle</u>. Even if the universe expands for ever it will cool, but at a decreasing rate. Intelligent creatures in the future would have sufficient time to succeed in learning how to transfer their 'software minds' into different hardware computer brains. As these machines increased in processing rate, infinite thought processing rates would be reached, which would correspond to immortality in Tipler's view. Eventually intelligence would fill the universe in a

giant computer network, as computers could also reproduce into subsequent generations. A god-like entity
would emerge. If the universe were closed, processing
rates would also continue to increase, and Tipler suggests that just prior to the big crunch the universe
would briefly contain the knowledge of everything and
become some sort of god too for an instant before
extinction!

Only God knows us completely; hence, any human
simulation will only ever be based on incomplete
information, and consequently will be an inadequate
copy.

Now these strange ideas beg many questions. First,
they underrate the nature of living things. It is by no
means clear that we can 'download' our minds as if we
were some fleshly computer (see Question 35). Our
minds are not merely accumulators of facts, or rational
intellects. They are the seats of emotions, desires, hopes
and ambitions bound up inextricably with our bodies.
Although in the future something might be simulated, it
would not be fully 'us', but a simulated 'us'. The
Christian hope of the resurrection envisages that we will
be resurrected as ourselves. Only God knows us completely, and he alone knows the secrets of our hearts
(Psalm 44:21); hence, any human simulation will only
ever be based on incomplete information, and consequently will be an inadequate copy. This is partly due to
physical limitations caused by the measuring problem
of quantum mechanics, however fast the computer (see
Question 16). Also, Tipler's god is a kind of giant intellect. The God of the Bible is far more than intellect. God

is not impassable as some Greek philosophers assumed, but one who cares (1 Peter 5:7), feels and has compassion (Hosea 11:8).

Secondly, given the limitations of mind transfer, could anything like this ever be done? In science fiction it appears easy, of course. For instance, all we need to do is to transport the living (sorry about those already dead, but this isn't the Christian hope here, you understand) and store them in an equivalent of the *Star Trek* 'pattern buffer', awaiting some future apotheosis! How much would be needed for just *one* person? Physicist Lawrence Krauss, in his book *The Physics of Star Trek*, computes it as equal to 10^{31} bits of information. This is equivalent to a stack of CD-ROMs a third of the radius of the galaxy! Unfortunately, it would take 2,000 times the life of the current universe to read at current rates![67]

In Tipler's resurrection, a giant computer will run simulations of all past lives. However, although God is omniscient, our memories are fallible. Only a poor representation of the former glories of those long dead will be possible. Although God does not abandon us (Psalm 94:19; Acts 2:27), this human world will. Such recreations, then, will be a pale reflection of what was once life, whereas in God's presence there will be life in all its fullness (1 Corinthians 2:9). The Christian hope seems a more credible alternative, in which the author of life renews us and we will dwell with him for ever. His understanding of us is more than we can know (Psalm 139:2), and is not beset with the physical limitations of knowledge-gathering. What will remain will be according to his mercy.

The Christian hope seems a more credible
alternative, in which the author of life renews us and
we will dwell with him for ever.

Sum-up

● There is little long-term hope for this universe. As it
  is, flesh and blood cannot inherit the kingdom of
  God.

● Some have tried to envisage a physical aspect to living again in human simulations of life. But because
  of the nature of the physical universe, this appears to
  be a poor and limited form of resurrection.

● The Christian hope looks beyond the running down
  of this world and towards the next.

45. If God knows about the future, how can we be truly free?

We live in the present, recall the past, and look forward to the future – a process which gives us the perspective that time flows. In the Bible the promises of God in the past give believers hope that God will look after them both in the present and in the future (e.g. Psalm 81:10). Yet there is an extra, if fleeting, dimension to its understanding of God that implies he knows the future in some way. The words of prophets do more than give a series of divine hopes. They declare things before they happen (Isaiah 42:9). Three times you will deny me, Jesus says to Peter, and he does (Matthew 26:34). The issue is not explored greatly, because the Bible details the way God works with his creation rather than engaging in philosophical speculation.

In the Bible there is a dimension to the description of God that implies he knows the future in some way.

The mathematical unit of time that physicists deal in can contrast strongly with the human experience of time. Time can pass 'in a flash'. Groucho Marx once dryly commented, 'Time wounds all heels!' The passage of time leads to our own passage of dust to dust, both psychologically and physically. Yet this century Albert Einstein's <u>Special Theory of Relativity</u> has given us some new insights into time. Time and space are linked so that time can be considered as effectively just another dimension. Events that happen occur not just at a particular place but at a particular time, depending on the observer. There is no absolute timescale, but only relative ones. 'The distinction between past, present and future is an illusion, though a persistent one,' said Einstein – all of time in this view exists in a sort of 'block'. Experiments have shown <u>relativity</u> to be correct beyond doubt, but does this mean we are effectively actors playing out some predetermined plot? Are Einstein's <u>metaphysical</u> insights correct?

'The distinction between past, present and future is an illusion, though a persistent one,' said Einstein.

Scientists who believe that the flow of time is real point to the history of the universe that has unfolded. Yet the scientific laws that describe the universe are often themselves without a sense to this direction of time. Quantum theory is an example of this (see Question 18). How then does the flow of time emerge such that we recognise the existence of cause and effect? The usual explanation is via the <u>Second Law of Thermodynamics</u>, which relates the order of events in terms of statistical likelihood (see Question 44). Nevertheless, scientists are still divided over which view of time is correct.

The block view of time bears a marked similarity to biblical ideas of eternity, and God's unchanging nature (James 1:17). But is this block view descriptive of the sort of eternity we mean when we talk about God? To God each event is of infinite preciousness – one day is as

a thousand years (2 Peter 3:8). Yet that finitude of engaging in time goes alongside a global view where a thousand years is as a day. God sees things 'spread out' in
his eternal present – all is immediate to him – yet the
biblical witness is that he can 'experience' time too. The
Christian understanding has always been that God is
somehow outside of time and beyond time, in the sense
that he is not an artefact of the universe (Numbers
23:19).

This difficulty in pinning down time has led to two
basic streams of Christian thought. In Calvinistic
thought, God's will in eternity governs contingent
events. God's omnipotence ensures that whatever happens, the drama of the universe is the outworking of his
will, a means to accomplish predetermined ends.
Human beings may have certain limited choices to
make, and are held responsible for them, but generally
speaking the die is already cast. The contrasting view,
called Arminianism, allows in essence completely free
choice over whether to turn to God or not.

In the Bible the words for eternity in Hebrew and
Greek both have a sense of time flowing. We can only
know of God's purposes with reference to our time
frame. That purpose includes the saving act of Christ, to
which each can respond so that they may become God's
chosen ones. Since God created space and time, and
came to save us in Christ, this suggests that we can
make real choices that determine the future. If not,
Christ's earthly ministry would be merely to complete
judgements on individuals that had already been decided upon. Our decisions too would be irrelevant. But in
his humanity, Christ himself made real choices (John
12:27); may we not do the same? If God knows the
future, he knows it at least to the extent that we can be

truly free in our actions to choose him, and he limits his omnipotence out of love for us, and respect for our freedom.

A more radical lack of divine foreknowledge is expressed in process theology, which describes God as a 'fellow-traveller in time' just like us. God would then be as ignorant of the future as we are. Certainties would be expressible as possibilities, but no more. God might only *perhaps* wipe away every tear from our eyes (cf. Revelation 21:4).

One of the difficulties in this kind of talk is the unwitting smuggling in of temporal concepts. We cannot say that in eternity God has already decreed something, because that word 'already' is a temporal word. Darting between temporal and eternal models will inevitably yield inconsistencies. The best we can say is that God, existing in time past, present and future, must be timelessly consistent in his character and in his covenant of divine permission for the universe (Genesis 1:22, 28). Even so, a notion of consistency is itself temporal, reflecting our inability to use our language reliably for eternal concepts.

The book of Revelation describes a symbol of Christ crucified in an image of a lamb slain being present 'from the foundation of the world' (Revelation 13:8, Authorised Version). Before 'the foundation of the world' there was effectively no time. Yet temporally the acts of a loving God reflect his will. Concentrating on commitment rather than freedom (the latter so valued today) may enable some further insights. In the Incarnation (see Question 40) we see something of God's commitment for us in time and space. He cannot and does not want to contract out of his commitment as creator. His eternal will reflects an unchanging commitment of love to his creation which allows it permission to become itself, and even make decisions that fall short of his wishes (Romans 3:23).

This divine permission allows God's creatures to enjoy real though limited freedom and a chance to genuinely respond to his call. We have seen how chaos theory (see Question 26) and quantum theory reveal a world where outcomes are not predictable. We instinctively feel free to make decisions, but cannot yet explain consciousness (see Question 31), although we recognise that these choices are often made from an input of upbringing and society's constraints.

Divine permission allows God's creatures to enjoy real though limited freedom and a chance to genuinely respond to his call.

The block view of time sees the universe as static. The God of eternity is unchanging, but nevertheless dynamic, and acting in his world. The block picture is a poor metaphor of God's timelessness, but the purely temporal view is not a complete description either. Rather God gives freedom as well as responsibility; he acts consistently in time according to his unalterable eternal nature.

Instead of dwelling on the difficulty of thinking about God knowing what is the future for us, the Bible gives us the confidence that his bidding will eventually prevail. This would suggest Arminianism is temporally true and that we each have a free choice whether to accept Christ or not (e.g. Acts 17:30), but perhaps Calvinism reflects the eternal changeless character of God who knows who are his chosen ones – something that we as time-bound creatures cannot discern (2 Timothy 2:19).

Sum-up

● Both science and religion have questioned whether past, present and future can in some way exist together in a 'block universe'. This goes against our subjective feelings of time 'flowing'.

● God's absolute power over the universe seems to be at risk if he invests his creatures with some say in their destiny. God's love allows it, however, so that human love may be returned.

● Whether we are truly free or not does not release us from responsibility for decisions we take in this world.

● If time is an illusion, then it is a persistent one for our universe, and one that allows divine action in time within the remit of an unchanging atemporal will.

FINAL HEADACHE QUESTIONS

Making sense of God and his world

46. Christians believe God is a Trinity – three in one. How can that make sense to a scientist?

Even in the Western world today, most people believe in God. But any astute enquirer will also ask the question, 'What is your God like?' In the Old Testament it is emphasised that God is one. He is without rival, and he transcends any image, be it physical or mental, that we can impose on him. Many religions such as Christianity, Judaism and Islam share such views. But if we say, for example, that God is merciful (Deuteronomy 4:31), then that mercy must be qualified. God's mercy cannot be exactly like ours, for our qualities of goodness and mercy are flawed.

Islam suggests that we cannot know Allah except through metaphor; we can know nothing of his <u>essence</u>. The Jewish people, the Bible explains, understood what God was like from what he did (Deuteronomy 4:35), and from how he revealed himself to the prophets (Exodus 34:6). But even the adjectives they used betray an anthropomorphic understanding. For example, the Bible describes God as speaking (Ezekiel 10:5), hearing the cries of his people (Psalm 140:6), and acting by his holy arm (Isaiah 52:10). We last only for three score years and ten (or thereabouts – Psalm 90:10), but God is everlasting (Isaiah 40:28). These attributes do not mean that God has a mouth or ears or an arm, or is somehow within space, or has a long retirement ahead! We may express views on God's personality, but that does not mean he is a mere person. An 'infinite' God is beyond comprehension by finite creatures. He is transcendent, and Lord of the universe.

We may express views on God's personality, but that does not mean he is a mere person.

God cannot be known by human knowledge as an object of our study, then, but only insofar as he reveals himself to us. We must humbly allow God to communicate his own nature to us. The Christian claims to know what he does about God, because God has made himself known in Jesus Christ. It is from this revelation, from data given to us both hazily in the Old Testament and more clearly in the New Testament in the person of Christ, that we can reliably picture what God is like.

Christians recognise that in Jesus we see exactly what this invisible God is like (Colossians 1:15). He is Immanuel, God with us (Matthew 1:23; see Question 40). The disciples whom Jesus called to follow him believed in the one God. But as they began to get to know their master, they recognised that he was someone who actually followed his Father's will. The work of God was seen in what he did (Matthew 11:4 – 6), and God's truth was heard in what he said (Luke 10:22). Even the most sceptical disciple, Thomas, recognised this after Jesus' resurrection (see Question 41): 'My Lord and my God!' he cried as he worshipped him (John 20:28).

Christians recognise that in Jesus we see what this invisible God is like.

At Pentecost Jesus sent 'another Counsellor', the Holy Spirit (John 14:16), to be with his followers (Acts 15:28). Their experience was of God revealed as Father, Son and Holy Spirit. Such data, of course, required analysis over a period of time. With regard to God, the church took several centuries to reach its conclusion that God is three in one – a Trinity; three persons in the one being of the Almighty. The early church was too busy proclaiming Jesus to be much involved with early speculation. They offered worship to Jesus because he had saved them (as God had saved the Jews in the Exodus from Egypt), and the indwelling Holy Spirit of God led them. The Trinity was an economic (experienced) trinity – it was what the evidence demanded in practice as well as in theory. In the relationship between God the Father and God the Son, they discovered an inclusive love that went beyond the personal, and drew them into the love of God through God the Spirit.

But is God really like this? Think for a moment about someone you know who is reliable. The person they truly are and how they act are compatible. Should God be any less than this? The Bible says that God is love (1 John 4:16), and back in the twelfth century there was a rediscovery of what this meant. We need this today because our society has devalued the word 'love' so that it implies only particular expressions of feelings and drives. A Christian thinker, Richard of St Victor (d. 1173), thought about what sort of love described God. Surely it should be the most complete love? And even before the creation it must have been more than self-love that in people is narcissism. God's love must be for another, and so Richard said he must be at least a duality of persons. But such love between two people can become exclusive unless there is a third person to share communally in complete love. Hence in the Trinity we see perfect love expressed. Richard's model of the Trinity says something not only about God's attributes but his essence too.

Can this make sense to a scientist? In many ways the scientist's <u>empirical</u> approach is exactly what forced these fiercely monotheist Jews to conclude that God really is like this! However strange a scientific model may seem, scientists are often forced to conclude that this is the way things are. The dual nature of light was doubted for a long time (see Question 16), but now although we realise we cannot picture it, scientists recognise that they have discovered something real. When theologians and scientists use metaphors and models, they apply them either qualitatively or quantitatively to relate new revelations about God and his creation, in order to reveal new insights (see Question 2).

The empirical approach is exactly what forced these fiercely monotheist Jews to conclude that God really is like this!

Christian teachers constantly looked for analogies that would make it easier to understand this relationship of Father, Son and Holy Spirit without dissolving the persons or making the one God into three gods. Physical analogies such as a single three-leafed clover, or three torches lit from one another provide examples. Relational analogies such as a lover, a beloved and the love between them are also used. Jesus' two great commandments (love of God and neighbour) relate self, neighbour and God to each other (Luke 10:27). A modern analogy might be between observer and observable, and the resultant outcome in quantum mechanics (see Question 18). St Paul reminds us that creation reflects its creator to an extent in both nature and intent (Romans 1:20).

Scientists have begun to learn to live with mysteries. The togetherness-in-separation of quantum particles is a particular one that points to this relational universe (see Question 17). Down the centuries Christians have done the same, relying on the fellowship of God as the Father upholding them, the Son saving them and the Holy Spirit transforming them. God exists in a relationship of mutual, social love and dependence that we can share through the work of Christ. It is a mystery too, but a reality and a relationship worth investing in.

Sum-up

● Without God's revelation we only guess what God is like.

● The witness of the Gospels is that God reveals himself and is experienced as Father, Son and Holy Spirit. Our knowledge of this is from the revelation of Jesus Christ in his earthly ministry, and a relationship of love that results from it.

● This century scientists have begun to realise that the world is stranger than they thought. There is no reason why God should not be so too as its creator.

47. Isn't science starting to play God? Aren't we opening a Pandora's box now it looks possible to gain genetic control over living creatures and even clone them?

Today the field of genetics is providing science with its greatest ethical questions ever. As we get nearer to manipulating the fundamental characteristics of life, and produce a growing number of genetically modified organisms (GMOs), be they plants or animals, scientists are beginning to recognise the need for guidance, so that neither technological capability nor commercial gain becomes the basis for scientific advance.

These concerns result from an increasing number of genetic advances, of which the most notable was the first <u>cloning</u> of a large mammal, Dolly the sheep, reported in February 1997. This had previously been thought impossible. The following month President Clinton ordered a widespread ban on government funding of human cloning in the USA. Great Britain and Germany have also banned it.

What is not generally realised, though, is that the reason for this experiment was essentially therapeutic. The researchers were looking at ways of producing complex proteins in sheep and cow's milk through genetic engineering. One such protein is called α_1-antitrypsin (AAT). Patients suffering from emphysema, which can have a genetic cause, need this protein to stop their lungs degenerating. Treatment requires about 200g per annum, which requires its extraction from huge quantities of valuable human blood. A small herd of sheep has been produced where the human <u>gene</u> sequence to produce this protein in humans has been inserted at the embryo stage. This is done in such a way that the modified cells specifically go to form milk-producing cells in the fully grown adult. The sheep's milk produces large quantities of AAT cheaply, which can then be extracted.[68] The cloning of Dolly at the Roslin Institute and PPL Therapeutics outside Edinburgh was an attempt to avoid losing these valuable cells, and having to start the process again in each generation.[69]

On a limited scale this would seem to be ethically acceptable. A similar use of micro-organisms such as bacteria to produce cheap insulin is one example of how genetic engineering can be effective on a controlled scale. But what of wider uses? What risks might be involved? Although mankind has employed selective breeding techniques for plants and animals over hundreds of years, these transgenic (meaning genes altered or introduced by humans into another living thing) plants and animals are something that nature could never produce. Evolution produces variety and increases ability to survive (see Question 23), whereas cloning leads to a narrowing of diversity. This might increase the risk of wholesale annihilation by disease, much as the French wine industry was nearly destroyed from the beetle-like phylloxera last century. Only bringing in diverse American bug-resistant vine strains and grafting onto them the few remaining European vines saved the industry.

Evolution produces variety and increases ability to survive, whereas cloning leads to a narrowing of diversity.

However, it is not only the issue of diversity, but also the use of animals as commodities that raises concerns. Leaner beef cattle or higher milk productivity in cows may satisfy commercial pressures, but run the risk of unnecessary suffering. We have a responsibility for animal welfare, even if some maintain that animals have few rights. A Christian perspective would be to recognise that animals have inherent worth to God, as a part of his creation. We cannot therefore impose our purposes upon them independently of their own God-given natures. Although we may battle against naturally occurring disease organisms, the beauty of higher orders of creation surely leads us to a different conclusion. Engineering an animal such that, for example, it were to be so corpulent that it could not move would be to deny that animal its God-given character, however lowly.

Also, current genetic techniques are crude, with much destruction of life. Rates of insertion of only around 1 per cent are usual (for Dolly, her birth arose from 430 attempts, with several abnormal foetuses being formed!). This is often because resultant gene placement and interactions with other surrounding genes produce non-viable embryos. Whatever our views on abortion and issues of when life begins, and whether embryos have 'rights', few would want to agree to such wastage of potential life.[70] The role of scientists should be to enhance the possibility of life, not reduce it in the desire for particularity.

The latter fact has led even some scientists to reject human cloning. Such sci-fi worries as cloned dictators are still far off, yet few countries have banned research. In December 1998 South Korean scientists reported they had possibly cloned human cells, though they stopped the experiment because of a government ban, so viability was not tested. But if cloning were possible, what would a cloned child be – a unique individual or a designed product? Would it effectively be made rather than begotten? Parental hopes are high for any newborn baby. Far more would be expected of a clone than of a natural child in terms of the choices to be made in life. We have already indicated how genes don't function in a prescriptive way (see Question 28), but through the high cost, a natural expectation would be for a real return and great disappointment would result if it did not materialise.

Such possibilities open up the question of whether the child has a right to genetic material from two parents. In the case of a Dolly-like clone produced from a husband's cell nucleus and a wife's egg, the result would effectively be a 'delayed' twin of the father! It might be possible, as in Dolly's case, that two females might produce the child. No 'father' need be involved. One of the human characteristics that God has allowed us is freedom. Having our own set of naturally acquired parental genes is surely part of a person being free.

One of the human characteristics that God has allowed us is freedom. Having our own set of naturally acquired parental genes is surely part of a person being free.

It may be that future medical boards permit cloning for therapeutic reasons (see also Question 43). Storage of cloned embryo cells might permit future growth of replacement organs that would automatically be compatible. This would raise problems of the status of the embryo. What must be uppermost in the mind of assessors is the inherent dignity of all human life. Christians will have serious doubts about a process that effectively uses a potential twin for spare parts.

Cloning tissue for therapeutic ends looks promising, though. Ethical assessment is beginning on the recently announced culturing of human embryonic stem cells that might allow growth of replacement defective cells. This requires initial use of foetal material, and there are ethical considerations over that, but the resulting cells can be engineered to be self-perpetuating. These undifferentiated cells can then be used to produce specific differentiated cells, such as heart or nerve cells, that do not regenerate, in order to repair damaged ones. Eventually this may be a stepping stone in learning how to reprogramme human cells to alleviate illness.

International co-operation is needed to avoid a slide into doing this research for the purposes of inquisitiveness masquerading as slender benefits. Many ethics boards are beginning to assess the responses, and these have both Christian input, in seeing humanity as stewards of God's creation, and input from those of other faiths. In the UK, the Human Fertilisation and Embryo Authority which licenses research, and the Human Genetics Advisory Commission that advises the government are bodies that already exist to regulate research.[71]

More pressing is the worry people have concerning the impact of genetic modification in foods. For example, tomatoes that are firmer and reach the supermarket in better condition can be produced by introducing genetic material that cancels out the manufacture of softening chemicals in the tomato. Crops have been engineered to carry bacteria-resistant genes in order to avoid the use of pesticide sprays, though paradoxically, this can also lead to the temptation of using more chemicals to yield even higher crop returns. Also, this 'good' has sometimes led the pests subsequently to develop a resistance that they otherwise would not have had. Nature adapts to our solutions and consequently different problems inevitably arise. This may not always be so, but the necessity for extensive trials is even more important where the likelihood of genetic material getting out into the biosphere becomes real. The initial higher price of such genetically modified seeds will also restrict use in third world countries where arguably they are needed more.

Generally, the public legitimately requires convincing over GMO production, especially in Great Britain following the BSE crisis. This is becoming a harder resistance for scientists to overcome, especially as food retailers recognise public resistance to novel foods and ban genetically modified components in them. Scientists may agree that modifications are minor, but there is a gap between an acceptance by the scientific community of the equivalence of such foods (that is, these novel foods pose no risk over 'normal' ones) and that of the wider, largely non-scientific, public. Assertions of authority are unlikely to be met with quiescence any more (see also Question 10).

Christians may wish a blanket ban on such work, believing it to be inherently wrong, yet almost all human achievements potentially have good or bad outcomes. The purpose of Christian input into regulatory agencies is that it brings the perspective that takes God's love of creation seriously, and therefore provides a source for moral values much needed in the world.

The purpose of Christian input into regulatory agencies is that it brings in God's perspective.

Mankind has played God consistently over the years as we 'subdue' nature. As we inevitably continue to do so we need God's perspective that respects and indeed loves creation. Our duties and responsibilities require more reflection of past insights into nature, lest we end up with a human sentimentality that arises largely from ignorance. As we rule the earth we need the wisdom of Solomon to deal in 'what is right and just and fair' (Proverbs 1:3), and a wisdom that seeks God's counsel (Job 15:8).

Sum-up

- We are on the verge of having genetic control over our environment as never before, far beyond what nature could produce.

- Cloning raises issues of what are the fundamental rights of creatures that are effectively being 'made' and not begotten. Ethical bodies seek to give guidelines, and assess what limits are to be imposed on scientific research. Christians have a duty to provide input into this assessment.

- Nature is responsive to our actions and this requires a greater wisdom if serious dangers are to be avoided.

48. Religion gets some way towards the truth and science some more. Why can't I just choose the bits I like?

Life is fragmented and compartmentalised today with little sense of destiny. The increasingly accepted concept of a distinction between public integrity and private behaviour is one pointer to this. Yet for the past several hundred years various philosophies (often dependent on scientific insight) have sought to provide grand unifying answers to the questions of life. Science has provided us with a large fragment of human understanding, but it does not represent all knowledge, and far less does it embrace all wisdom.

Science has provided us with a large fragment
of human understanding, but it does not
represent all knowledge, and far less does
it embrace all wisdom.

The backlash of this realisation has led to an obvious conclusion. Science cannot give us the big picture, a metanarrative for the world. Previously, religions had done so, but many scientists convinced people that God had been banished by science (or rather, by those who wished to promote humanity to his place). Therefore, why not dethrone science too? This new sense has often been given the label postmodern. Tired of the confusing and often contradictory messages of the biased wisdom of this world, the new catchphrase could be expressed as 'Dare to disregard'. Postmodern people are suspicious people.

Suspicion breeds isolationism, however. 'Once bitten, twice shy' would be a favourite motto for many people today. Humanity's long search for a meaning in life for all has therefore given way to individuals seeking meaning for themselves. Often, trying to make sense of the world has given way to despair and a goal to do nothing more than just survive as best one can.

Now suspicion does not necessarily imply rejection. Postmodern people are cautious people, but they are realists. They do not dismiss the discoveries of science, nor consider that those who profess religious insight are wrong. Instead they suggest that faith in God and belief in the power of science are simply two options among many. They consider that they can make up their mind as they see fit – not as part of a rational group that agrees, but as autonomous individuals. In a world dominated by advertising, it is said that everyone has a vested interest, so why not just make up a portfolio of your own beliefs? Anyone can have faith, but now it is a personalised, private faith. Postmodernism is the result of previous philosophies that raised the importance of subjectivity; its clarion call is therefore 'You decide'. The question 'Is it true?' has become 'Is it true for you?' What you *feel* is more significant than what you *know*.

Therefore, attempts to evangelise others with meta-narratives, whether it is belief in God or in science, are considered dictatorial. People are suspicious of authority figures whom they know have failed them in the past. Yet both science and religion are replete with proponents who still assume that their message will be heard because as gurus they have a right to be heard.

This is no longer so. Objectivity has become the slave of subjectivity.

Now a pick 'n' mix philosophy of life is remarkably easy to obtain, especially in a busy world with mass communication; in fact, busy lives mean it is often the only way to glean wisdom. A society that grazes on its physical food will inevitably do so on its mental fare too. Both science and religion have difficult concepts and they are often not readily or quickly understood. For instance, the Alpha course is a highly popular Christian basics course across the world. It comprises some fourteen hours of teaching over a similar number of weeks. And that is just the basics! Equally, becoming a scientist takes years of study. Why not just ignore the hard grind, avoid science A-levels and go for something simpler? After all, it's suggested, does it really make any difference what you believe?

A society that grazes on its physical food will inevitably do so on its mental fare too.

Yet it is worth asking whether we can do this with integrity in the case of either science or Christianity. We may respect the value of individuals, but it does matter what a person believes. It must at least be rational and coherent to some extent. For example, if you don't believe that when you drive too fast around a sharp bend the momentum will force your car to continue in a straight line, then you could end up leaving the road and possibly killing yourself! In other words, there are laws or consequences that follow on logically from what we already know to be so. Not all beliefs are relative or can be easily disconnected from each other.

**There are laws or consequences that follow on
logically from what we already know to be so. Not
all beliefs are relative.**

The message of both science and the Bible is that our
universe has a history that has unfolded over millions of
years. Scientists have discovered objective and coherent
sets of laws from which they seek to explain new happenings. These disciplines are rooted in history and
form narratives that yield truth (see Question 2). So it is
not possible to take out bits of each and make separate
value judgements on them. You cannot believe in a God
of love who does not also take justice or righteousness
seriously (or that love is a sham), just as you cannot take
the phenomenon of radiocarbon dating away from science (because you might believe the earth is only 6,000
years old) and retain a consistent story of the universe.
Partial beliefs are ultimately incoherent beliefs. Major
events such as the resurrection or the genetic tree of life
have knock-on effects (see Questions 41 and 22).

Partial beliefs are ultimately incoherent beliefs.

Does this mean that science and the Christian faith
will continue to wane in their ability to influence society? The answer is a conditional no. But the condition is
that science and religion must recognise that a lack of a
metanarrative does not mean that nothing is believed.
People are still anxious to find truth and meaning in the
world around. And both science, via its technological
wizardry, and Christianity, when lived out faithfully by

its adherents following the gospel message, can best do that when they touch lives.

People cannot live for long without coherence, and ultimately this is what science and religion provide. People may believe in anything today, but they won't believe in it for long. Crop circles or the supposed power of crystals does not amount to a great deal compared to the concrete and coherent advances in science, and the millions of lives given meaning by knowing Christ. A faith that really changes lives will become as valued as an incubator that saves the life of someone's child. It is no surprise that the testimonies of individuals are so popular when screened by the media, whether in religious or science programmes. Men and women need to build metanarratives again, and both science and faith can provide sturdy bricks for construction.

Men and women need to build metanarratives again, and both science and faith can provide sturdy bricks for construction.

At best, both science and religion are not about compelling belief, but are about persuasion. They are least attractive when being authoritarian. Historically, education has tended to favour compulsion, as it is an easier route for teachers to travel. But science is so often at its most compelling when it is in the business of discovering something new about the world, just as faith is a challenge and an invitation to 'taste and see that the Lord is good' (Psalm 34:8).

Sum-up

- Society is fragmenting. Its advice to people today is to make up their own minds on everything. However, they still seek meaning and purpose to their lives.

- Metanarratives, such as those offered by science and religions, are suspect.

- However, both science and the Christian faith represent coherent bodies of understanding that cannot be taken piecemeal.

- Therefore, because people still want to have a coherent set of beliefs, science and the Christian faith will have to assist in rebuilding this by persuasion and giving help in the lives of individuals.

49. At school we did experiments detailing method, observations and conclusions. How can that experimental approach apply to Christianity?

There is a common fear among many scientists that believing in God is tantamount to committing intellectual suicide. The previous chapters of this book have spent some time looking at the twentieth-century revolution in science and explain how belief in God is more possible now than at any time in the last several hundred years.

Yet the suspicion may still be that although God may indeed exist, there is still uncertainty as to what he is like. The greatest philosophers have discussed what he is like over several millennia and have not got very far. Some have even reduced God to being an artefact of linguistic analysis! The best way, of course, to get to know God and to know about him would be to meet him. Then you could really discover what he is like. At times of national calamity even the people of Israel wished for his presence (Psalm 144:5); they wanted a tangible God.

The best way to get to know God would be to meet him.

The biblical answer to how to know God is quite clear. The author of the letter to the Hebrews puts it this way:

In the past God spoke to our forefathers through the prophets at many times and in various ways, but in these

last days he has spoken to us by his Son, whom he appoint-
ed heir of all things, and through whom he made the universe. The Son is the radiance of God's glory and the exact
representation of his being, sustaining all things by his
powerful word. After he had provided purification for sins,
he sat down at the right hand of the Majesty in heaven.
(Hebrews 1:1–4)

The doctrine is staggering. God communicates not in a
speech, or a philosophy, or an ethic, but in a person. Not
some life force, cosmic energy, world spirit, or other
vague notion, but in a tangible human being. 'Anyone
who has seen me has seen the Father,' Jesus once said to
a questioning disciple (John 14:9). His challenge is for
people to examine his life.

Science is a powerful tool for examining the physical
world. From an initial observation a scientist produces a
hypothesis to explain it. He usually goes from this specific observation to create a general model of what is
happening; this is called <u>induction</u> (see also Question 2).
A good scientific model will have some predictive
power that enables him to design further specific experiments to test the new theory. If the experiment produces
observations that do not fit with the model, then the theory needs revision, and the whole cycle begins again.
Refinement leads to a tighter grasp on reality.

How might this tool be used in this case? Few scholars
now deny that Jesus really existed or suggest that the
records in the Gospels are cleverly made-up stories.
Look at his life then and his teaching. Start with the
Sermon on the Mount in Matthew's Gospel chapter 5. It
talks about righteousness and mercy and purity. It talks
about not escalating conflict. It talks about loving your
enemies. After two millennia we know it needs to be our

goal, but as a society we still struggle to follow Jesus' teaching. Look too at what he claimed about himself, and above all at the character and integrity of the man. 'By their fruit you will recognise them,' he said (Matthew 7:16). Today people are rightfully hot on integrity. 'Do as I say; don't do as I do' has never carried much force. It didn't when we were children and it doesn't now. Yet that Sermon on the Mount fits as you read the life of Jesus. Today, public figures are often caught out. Some sin emerges in their lives. But it did not with Jesus. Those closest to him saw a sinless man. Even his enemies recognised his incorruptibility (Matthew 22:16). He can say, 'I am the light of the world' (John 9:5) and, 'I am the way and the truth and the life' (John 14:6), and it does not seem out of place for him. If you or I tried that we would be exposed in an instant (probably by our spouse or a close friend!). But Jesus' character accords with his claims and his teaching.

The method: look at Jesus' life.
The observations: his character accords with his claims and his teaching.

Look too at his followers. He not only said, 'I am the light of the world,' but he told his followers, 'You are the light of the world' (Matthew 5:14). Early Christians had no problem with that verse (even though some may find it uncomfortable today). Their faith led them to endure terrible persecution, for in their ordinary lives they had discovered the extraordinary claims of Christ to be true. By his resurrection they could know him and therefore recognised that he had saved them. One such man was a person called Attalus. He was tried and he confessed to being a Christian in Lyons, France in AD 177. His torturers tried to force him to worship the emperor by sitting him in an iron chair heated up to scorching heat. He died burned but refusing to worship anyone but Jesus. He knew he had met with God; a mere Roman emperor wouldn't do in his place!

Assess also the evidence recorded in the Gospels, for its authors have already done the experiment. All good scientists will want to evaluate the results and come to their own conclusions. Faith would not be faith if it were compulsion. Rather faith is a matter of trust. Anselm, Archbishop of Canterbury in 1093, recognised the need for a leap of faith when he said, 'I believe in order to understand.' Such a route might seem a bit drastic for someone unsure, although even the basis of science is not totally secure; the mathematical roots of science must also be taken on trust (see Question 8).

The Christian faith is about grace and forgiveness. Christians believe that Jesus died that they might be forgiven. They should act first of all, then, as people who are thankful for that fact, and are changed or are being changed by it (Romans 12:2). One of the best evangelists in Britain became a Christian in his middle teens. Determined not to be fooled, he observed several friends who claimed they were Christians. Did this faith make any difference? He observed them over several months (his parameters for the experiment were well chosen) and he found that it did. He saw they had something he did not. It was not that they were perfect, but he noticed the differences that there were.[72]

You may choose to do the same. Try looking at what differences there are in people who have recently become Christians. Ask them about the difference believing in Jesus makes, and who they think he is. It is perfectly acceptable to challenge them if their lifestyle doesn't match up to what they profess, for the Bible challenges all Christians to holy living (2 Peter 3:11). But in true scientific tradition make sure the conclusions you reach are honest. Some years ago a professor of organic chemistry (which investigates the chemistry of carbon compounds) in the USA was in sharp dispute over the nature of a particular type of chemical bond. Two plausible models existed for it and he was strongly in favour of one of them. Many times he did the experiment that would determine the answer. At a conference he showed a single result that just about confirmed his view. His colleagues were surprised, as they tended to think the other model was on balance more likely. A few months later his students spilled the beans. He had repeated the experiment over 300 times until just the right result came up. The other results all favoured what he didn't want to believe!

A good scientist makes observations, looks at the results and draws conclusions, but does not fight shy of them. Evidence for the Christian faith rests not only on observations of the behaviour of Christians, of course, but on the person of Christ (see Questions 40 and 41). If the conclusion is that Christianity and its life-transforming claims are untrue, then an enquirer can forget it. But if Christianity is true and potentially life transforming, then a good scientist must do something about it and consider the call of Jesus to follow him and become a disciple.

A good scientist makes observations, looks at the results and draws conclusions, but does not fight shy of them.

The great scientists of history have been those who had the courage to stand out from the crowd and commit themselves to a new idea that subsequently revolutionised the world. In 1941 Sir William Bragg, Nobel Prize winner for his determination of the structure of crystals by X-rays said: 'Science is experimental, moving forward step by step, making trial and learning through success and failure. Is not this also the way of religion, especially the Christian religion? The writings of those who preach the religion have from the very beginning insisted that it is to be proved by experience.'[73] That experience is found by a commitment to take a step of faith in our own continuing 'experiment' of life.

Sum-up

● Science is indeed a process of method, observation and conclusion.

● Scientific pursuit may make us come to conclusions we had not thought likely. Great scientists have often been those unafraid to go against the flow for what they believed to be true.

● If we are honest, then this will lead the enquirer to examine the claims of Jesus Christ, and not fight shy of conclusions that lead towards the truth (John 8:32).

50. What can the Christian faith say to scientists today when technology is progressing and religion seems to be stuck in the past?

Science has uncovered a marvellously constructed world. Within its delicate balances, awesome creatures have emerged from matter and energy that are equally strange and wonderful. Science deliberately limits its field of investigation to tangible phenomena, and so its conclusions are limited also. But it is, nevertheless, a very powerful tool for discerning causal links in a world of undeniable complexity.

Science deliberately limits its field of investigation to tangible phenomena, and so its conclusions are limited also.

Religions such as Christianity might at first appear to be hopelessly locked into the past. But the writers of the New Testament did not take a parochial view of events. Their claims for Jesus as Lord went beyond the belief that he was just a local Saviour for the Jewish people suffering under Roman oppression. They were of a person who is eternally alive in whom all past, present and future finds its meaning. In their early worship of the living Jesus, the apostles began to realise that Christ was Lord of all (e.g. Revelation 4:11–5:6). The discovery of Jesus risen from death (see Question 41) changed defeated disciples into bold people who would transform the world with the gospel. Theirs were not the actions of hallucinating or mentally ill men and women, but of pioneers who have discovered the truth. The disciples were the greatest 'come-back kids' of all time.

The discovery of Jesus risen from death changed defeated disciples into bold people who would transform the world with the gospel.

Many social developments have failed the test of time: economic policies that favour a market-place approach to business that mean the weak or the unfortunate go to the wall; medical advances that are heralded but never quite materialise; political promises before elections that tarnish quickly in the realities of office; permissiveness that failed the last generation replaced by stimulants that will fail this generation. All are mediated by fallible human souls and have failed to save us.

What sort of God should we believe in then? Certainly science shows that in fashioning the universe God took great time and care over its inception (see Questions 11–13 and 22). It is not an arbitrary world, but a rational one (see Questions 4 and 16). God made a good world and creatures fit for a universe of change (see Questions 23–25). He is a being who has built a flexible world that can have real freedom from the roots up and yet is not chaotic (see Questions 17–19 and 26). Consequently, our whole being can have a largely independent existence (see Questions 27–29, 37–38 and 48) so that we can choose to recognise him or not in how we seek after understanding (see Questions 1– 4 and 33). With our conscious minds, though, we can think God's rational thoughts after him (see Questions 5–8). As humans we are made of the building-blocks of creation, yet we have the marvellous ability to think beyond it to spiritual matters (see Questions 20–21 and 42). We have a God who is personal, a God of relationships, and in whose image we are made (see Questions 13, 31 and 39). Science has uncovered the importance of the relational, in terms of both time and space, and biology (see Questions 15 and 45). God, then, is caring, gracious, rational, personal and loving, and is calling us into a relationship with him.

Yet God knows our frailty and our wilful ways, even wanting to be like him, knowing good, but unlike him choosing evil (see Questions 36, 43 and 47). On the road to Damascus, St Paul discovered that the real lasting solution to the world's ills was found in this wandering preacher from Nazareth, not just for his time, but for all time. In the Incarnation God became in a marvellous way fully one of us (see Questions 40 and 46), for he is a condescending God, not aloof from the world. Paul became aware that he was wrong about what God was like, and that what he had heard of Jesus was true. His picture of God underwent a paradigm shift after meeting the risen Christ. Paul was not so much convinced intellectually as convicted personally. We cannot readily uncouple the one from the other, even in science (see Question 49). The meeting with Christ led him to have his life transformed, for that is Christ's business: human nature can be renewed, and attitudes, lifestyle and prejudices can be changed. Former hatreds are turned into love. Technology may progress, but Christianity addresses human nature, which is what really stays much the same. We have realised that science is not the salvation of the world and can never be. It needs careful handling, for fallible humans perform it (see Questions 10, 15 and 47). Finally, even though our universe has no happy ending, God's love offers us a renewed world, where suffering is no more (see Questions 14 and 44).

I hope and pray that these questions and answers may convince you that embracing the Christian faith will not cause you to lose a passion for science, or the search for truth. Truth matters today just as much as in the past. In this life, weighing up the evidence inevitably leads to a point of decision. Many scientists have been drawn to the probability of a divine mind behind the universe. Cosmologist Paul Davies said, 'Science provides a surer path to God than religion'; whereas, in fact, Jesus provides a surer path to God than religion. One is the revelation of the incredible universe to us, while the other is the self-revelation of its incredible creator. A relationship with him is not about testing in a coldly objective, scientific way, but about entrusting one's life to God in a very subjective and personal manner. But it is one that is equally real nonetheless. Scientists are not afraid of asking questions and finding answers, but neither must they be afraid of addressing the consequences.

Scientists are not afraid of asking questions and finding answers, but neither must they be afraid of addressing the consequences.

A man called John once met the living Jesus in a vision, in which the wavering people in a town called Laodicea were asked to make a decision. Jesus said, 'Here I am! I stand at the door and knock. If anyone hears my voice and opens the door, I will come in and eat with him, and he with me' (Revelation 3:20). That offer is open to all, scientist and non-scientist alike. It is a knock on the door that must be answered.

Concluding prayer

Father God, Lord of the universe, forgive me when I see the wonders of creation but fail to see you as the wonderful creator. Give me a vision of the hope that you promise for your world, created through and redeemed by the death of your Son Jesus, that I too may have hope in this life and be part of the one to come. In Jesus' name. Amen.

Glossary of Scientific and Philosophical Terms

Algorithm: a means of computation or problem-solving by using a set of rules.

Anthropy, Anthropic Principle (in Greek *anthropos* means 'man'): the idea (in several different forms) that our universe is finely balanced in the process of becoming as we see it today, such that carbon-based life forms evolved because of such precision.

Axiom: a principle that is taken to be true without proof at the start of an argument.

Billion: here a thousand million.

Black hole: a collapsed burnt-out star that has such a huge gravitational attraction that neither matter nor even light can escape. It is likely that a massive black hole exists at the centre of our galaxy. Stephen Hawking proposed a means by which black holes can 'evaporate' as they capture material.

<u>Cognition, cognitive</u>: the act of someone knowing or perceiving something.

<u>Chromosomes</u>: these are found in living cells. They are composed of <u>DNA</u> and proteins, and divided into components called <u>genes</u>. The cells of each species contain a specific number of chromosomes, which in animals and more complex plants occur as pairs. Reproductive cells have only half the number of chromosomes of ordinary cells. In reproduction, pairs of such cells (sperm and egg cells) combine, making new cells with the correct number of chromosomes and hence a new generation.

<u>Clone, cloning</u>: a process of non-sexual reproduction. For Dolly the sheep, an egg cell had its nucleus (containing <u>DNA</u>) replaced by that from a dormant udder cell of an adult ewe. Not all of Dolly's DNA was identical to that of her 'mother' ewe, unlike in the case of identical twins. Not all of a cell's DNA is in the nucleus, but some is also in the <u>mitochondria</u> outside it. The other method nature itself employs of embryo cloning involves the splitting of the fertilised cells as they begin to divide. Identical twins form. Cloning of this sort is sometimes done in animal breeding, and cows and other higher mammals have also been reported as being cloned, but research is severely limited legally on human embryos.

<u>Critical realist, critical realism</u>: our models of reality can only ever make good guesses as to what really exists.

<u>Deduction</u>: guessing particular happenings from a general law.

<u>Determinism, deterministic</u>: the notion that every event

has a cause which follows scientific laws and is not subject to contingency, so that if a cause exists, then the event will always follow. This can be used to promote the idea that God cannot act in his universe, and that it is not 'open' to his working.

DNA, RNA: deoxyribonucleic acid and ribonucleic acid. Two classes of long chain helical molecules called nucleic acids that pass on hereditary characteristics and provide from their particular structure the means by which specific proteins are built in living cells.

Ego: that part of the personality in Freud's view which linked the person and the outside world. The basic drives and wishes in the unconscious form the id, and the third moralising counterpart is the superego.

Electromagnetic force: see Four forces of nature below.

Empirical: deriving knowledge from doing experiments or using one's senses.

Enlightenment: an eighteenth-century intellectual movement stressing human reason and individualism.

Entropy: a measure of the disorder of any physical system. In any isolated system the entropy will increase over time until equilibrium conditions are reached.

Essence: the reality underlying what we might observe in someone or something.

Four forces of nature: there are four basic forces in the universe. Electrical charge (+/-) and magnetic forces are part of the same electromagnetic force. It is a force 'carried' by particles called photons. Photons of different energy exist as visible light, microwave radiation, X-rays and so on. The photon has no mass at rest, but has energy (try sitting under a sun-ray lamp to feel it!). The second force is the weak nuclear force. This operates over a short distance and was discovered as part of radioactive decay and is the means by which heavier particles decay into weak ones. Because it is such a short-range force, the force particle (called a W or a Z) is correspondingly massive. The strong nuclear force is what binds quarks together in threes to form protons and neutrons and similar (heavier) particles. The strong force is very short range and particles called gluons bind quarks together according to known rules. The force is such that even the repulsion of similar charged particles in the atom's nucleus is overcome to give a stable atomic nucleus. Gravity is the fourth and weakest force, but because it is not limited in distance, it eventually overcomes all other forces in the universe. Particles called gravitons have not yet been seen.

General Theory of Relativity: this was Einstein's theory that linked gravitation with his earlier Special Theory of Relativity. Gravitational attraction is equivalent to acceleration and is the result of the curvature of space-time.

Genes: molecules found in the cells of our bodies that form the foundations for our inherited characteristics. Groups of them form chromosomes.

Genotype: the sum total of an organism's genetic make-up. As they operate in the living creature they go to make up the phenotype.

<u>Induction, inductive method</u>: concluding general laws from specific events.

<u>Inflation</u>: a process of very rapid expansion in the life of the universe, probably of the order of a factor of some 10^{40}! Although not properly understood, this process would eliminate some problems arising from a simple Big Bang expansion. The main one was why the universe was devoid of massive particles called magnetic monopoles (particles equivalent to a single pole of a magnet). If inflation hadn't occurred, then such particles would be as prevalent as the matter we see today, and hence they would have triggered an early end in a Big Crunch (and hence no mankind). It was also suggested that inflation might not stop at exactly the same time everywhere and small fluctuations in the value might be observed in the background radiation found everywhere in the universe. In fact, fluctuations were seen in 1992 by NASA's COBE space telescope, strengthening the case for inflation having happened.

<u>Metanarrative</u>: a grand view of events that seeks meaning and gives interpretations to show how history and current events should be read.

<u>Metaphysical</u>: ideas that go beyond the physical to analyse it in terms of deeper meaning – literally 'after physics'.

<u>Mitochondria</u>: bodies within cells of creatures that use oxygen in the breakdown of food to energy. Mitochondria perform the last part of this process very efficiently.

<u>Mutation</u>: a change in the genetic make-up of a living cell, which may be caused by external factors such as radiation. Mutations can often produce non-viable cells which die.

<u>Neurones, or neurons</u>: specialised body cells in our nervous system that convey electrochemical impulses. The cells are spiky in appearance and the 'spikes' either receive or send signals. Some spikes can be as much as a metre in length.

<u>Ontology</u>: insight into the nature of being, of what something inherently is. Epistemology is a frequently related concept to it, which is the study of what we can know.

<u>Phenotype</u>: observable characteristics of the organism that arise (see <u>genotype</u>).

<u>Positivists, positivism</u>: a philosophy that dismisses all metaphysical and religious ideas as meaningless (sometimes termed logical positivism).

<u>Paradigm, paradigm shift</u>: a paradigm is a raft of concepts, methods of getting information, beliefs and interpretations held by a society in any particular subject. A paradigm shift is where these are fundamentally upset and are interpreted afresh. Philosopher Thomas Kuhn suggested this in 1962.

<u>Postmodern (-ism)</u>: a rather flexibly defined word. Proponent Jean-François Lyotard has related it to right-side brain functions of artistry and play. Also it is the idea that former worldviews are not all-encompassing.

Your truth is your truth, and mine is mine. Neither must claim superiority over the other in authority or authenticity. Diversity rather than consensus rules. The truth claims of both science and religion are doubted because they claim to be absolutes.

Quanta, quantum (theory): a scientific model that explains events in the microscopic world by realising that energy comes in little packets called quanta.

Quarks: constituents of nuclei of atoms found in threes. Two quarks can also bind to form a class of particles called mesons. There are six types in all.

Realism, realist: classically, realism is the assertion of the independent existence of objects in their own right, or in older (medieval) philosophies that abstract concepts about them have real existence.

Relativity (see General Theory of Relativity and Special Theory of Relativity).

RNA (see DNA).

Second Law of Thermodynamics: comes from the observation that heat cannot be transferred from a body at a lower to a higher temperature. As systems tend to equilibrium they tend to maximum values of disorder defined by the term entropy. There are in fact four laws of thermodynamics in all. The zeroth law (it's called that as it in effect predefines the others) defines temperature, and the first equates heat and work as forms of energy. The third law identifies the lowest temperature that can be physically obtained as Absolute

Zero, -273.15 degrees Celsius.

Special Theory of Relativity: one of the problems of pre-Einstein science was that laws differed depending on the speed you were going. Einstein explained how laws were the same, independent of how fast you were going, but only when you realised that the speed of light was a constant value independent of how fast you went. This changed completely the absolute nature of time and space, and linked the two inextricably together in what he called a continuum. Space-time became relative to each observer. As you went at a faster speed, time slowed down, distances decreased and things increased in mass by an amount equivalent to the energy of the moving body $E=mc^2$. The effects are small at the slow speeds we normally travel at.

Species: a group of living creatures which is unable through genetic or geographical restriction to interbreed with another group. Divisions are not always clear with extinct species.

Standard Model: this interlocking theory is based upon experiment and considers how matter and forces interact. Since in quantum mechanics particles can be considered as waves and vice versa, so forces can be viewed as being mediated by the interaction or exchange of different force particles. All matter, it is thought, is made up of two sorts of matter called leptons and quarks. Earlier this century when the atom was split it was found to contain a small nucleus with a positive electric charge at the centre of orbiting negative particles called electrons. Electrons are an example of leptons, and the nucleus comprises both protons (with the positive electric charge) and neutrons (no electric charge). The latter are each made from three <u>quarks</u>. Six leptons and six quarks have been identified; they can be grouped into three generations – the heavier two generations decay into the lightest (first generation) ones. The universe's stable matter, then, is made from electrons and the lightest quarks. All the particles suggested by this standard model have been seen directly or indirectly.

<u>Strong Nuclear Force</u> (see <u>Four forces of nature</u> above).

<u>Superstring theory</u>: a multi-dimensional theory that describes matter as made up not of point particles but as tiny one-dimensional 'strings' that vibrate or rotate, so producing all we see today. They are too small to be detected but mathematically get close to unifying some of the disparate laws of nature we see.

<u>Weak Nuclear Force</u> (see <u>Four forces of nature</u> above).

Notes

1 See further results reported in *The Daily Telegraph* of 3rd April 1997, and popular science journals around then.

2 In October 1998 the papal encyclical *Fides et Ratio* (Faith and Reason) acknowledged that the unity of truth is a fundamental premise of reasoning. Galileo declared explicitly that the two truths of faith and science cannot contradict each other: 'Sacred Scripture and the natural world proceed equally from the divine Word, the first as dictated by the Holy Spirit, the second as a very faithful executor of the commands of God.' This quotation of Galileo shows how the modern church wishes to explore the necessary unity between faith and reason.

3 An anti-sickness sedative introduced in the late 1950s (and withdrawn in 1962) that caused foetal malformation. Currently usage for other illnesses is returning in some countries.

4 Peter W. Atkins, *Creation Revisited* (Penguin, 1992), p.109.

5 Like any good theory, Einstein's had predictive power and suggested experiments that would demonstrate his ideas. When some were done they were found to be correct. By this means Einstein had got a little further than Newton.

6 The normal role of prions is apparently to stop brain degradation. Mutation stops this process and the animal's brain degrades. It appears that offal from sheep with a prion-based

brain disease called scrapie, when fed to cattle, allowed the mutated prion protein to infect cattle, and mutate its prion protein, causing BSE (Bovine Spongiform Encephalopathy). The mutated cattle prion, having a slight similarity to human prion protein, could subsequently infect people, leading to CJD (Creutzfeld-Jakob disease).

7 In the USA bracelets with WWJD (What Would Jesus Do?) inscribed on them have become very popular. Look at Deuteronomy 6:8 to see a similar means of remembering God's word in the Old Testament. In Jesus we have his presence as the living Word.

8 Stephen W. Hawking, *A Brief History of Time* (Bantam, hardback edition, 1988), p.141 (paperback edition, 1995), p.157.

9 Roger Penrose, *The Large, the Small, and the Human Mind* (Cambridge University Press, 1997), p.48. This special state characterises our sense of time flow experienced as an increase of entropy.

10 Stephen W. Hawking, *A Brief History of Time* (Bantam, 1988), p.175.

11 Keith Ward, *God, Chance and Necessity* (Oneworld, Oxford, 1996), p.111. A readable account of Superstring theory can be found in *Beyond Einstein* by Michio Kaku and Jennifer Thompson (Oxford University Press, 1997).

12 In November 1998 astrophysicists found evidence of a possible earth-size planet by looking for reduction in a distant star's brightness as the planet went across its face. Other planets have been found by studying a wobbling effect on a star's motion, but these would indicate massive planets less suited to life.

13 Warm-blooded birds also probably developed from small dinosaurs, it is now thought. Characteristics such as large brains and heavy skulls for protection would be counter-productive for flight.

14 Pre-millennium tensions and the unfriendly alien races depicted in films such as *Starship Troopers* and *Alien* reflect society's current uncertainties. Alienation and the consequent fear of what the future holds are endemic in the

Western world that is losing touch with its spiritual roots.

15 See also the whole section of Ephesians 1:3 –14. This passage is a meditation on the universality of Christ's work and its benefits.

16 Oxygen was a product of the life of primitive algae-like marine plant cells called cyanobacteria. With a breathable atmosphere, dry land became inhabitable about 350 million years ago. Without them we would never have existed.

17 Sir Fred Hoyle suggested that amino acids might be carried around the universe in the frozen bodies of comets!

18 Full title: *On the Origin of Species by Means of Natural Selection or the Preservation of Favoured Races in the Struggle for Life.*

19 An excellent summary of what leading churchmen of the day actually believed is provided by Michael Roberts in *The Church Times,* 17th October 1997.

20 *Yom,* the Hebrew for 'day' means most often a literal day (Genesis 1:5), but also, much more rarely, a longer time marking an event (e.g. Numbers 9:22). However, other questions arise about what is being done by such an interpretation, and whether the author of Genesis would have recognised this (see Question 25).

21 Biologist Stephen Gould has suggested that there are in fact long periods of little change followed by rapid large ones. This is called 'punctuated equilibria', rather than Darwin's gradualism. Although Gould would not subscribe to a purposeful evolution, it is easy to ascribe such changes to being instances of God's action.

22 Evolution is time-consuming. Its rates of change are largely unknown, so assertions that a given (large) number of improbable steps will happen over a specific time are conjectural.

23 Michael J. Behe, *Darwin's Black Box* (Free Press, 1996).

24 Non-functioning bits of the evolving mousetrap also have to be kept in place (with no advantage over many more random assemblies) awaiting completion of every part, Behe points out. The probability of this is tiny. Behe's thesis has attracted some controversy in the scientific community.

25 The Hebrew word *bara'* is used of God creating in Genesis 1:1

and elsewhere (Psalm 51:10; 102:18; Jeremiah 31:22). Its focus is upon God doing a new thing, apparently contrasting what no other god nor man could do. It is not said what God creates out of – other words are used to define this (e.g. Genesis 2:7; 2:22). Creation out of nothing is part of later insight (John 1:3).

26 Modern Bible translations reflect this in the use of the term 'the man' rather than 'Adam'.

27 S.A. Tishkoff, *et al.*, *Science*, 8 March 1996, have suggested a single small group originated in NE Africa from mutation frequency in different world groups. The Eve hypothesis comes from studies of mother/child mitochondrial DNA, suggesting a 'genesis' around 150,000+ years ago. Genetic markers on male Y chromosomes independently suggest a date of a similar order. Allan J. Day, *Science and Christian Belief*, vol. 10.2, 1988, pp.115–143. Human-like beings appear to have arisen around 4 to 6 million years ago. Professor Sam Berry has recently independently suggested a similar scenario and coined the phrase *homo divinus*, 'created' as God revealed himself to an historical Adam and Eve. The genetic genesis of homo sapiens would be earlier than the spiritual genesis of Adam and Eve but we note (in Question 28) how the genotype does completely specify the phenotype. It would also explain where Cain found a wife! R. J. Berry, *Science and Christian Belief*, vol II.I, 1999, pp.29–49.

28 *Philosophical Essay on Probability* (1814).

29 This often meant writing equations that were linear; that is, directly proportional to some cause. Chaos Theory explores non-linear, dynamic systems.

30 An example of a chaotic system producing stability is the Great Red Spot on the surface of the planet Jupiter that has lasted for at least 330 years to our knowledge!

31 *Meditations on First Philosophy* (1641).

32 For example, compare Revelation 20:4, 'soul', and Luke 24:46 or James 2:26, 'spirit'. First Thessalonians 5:23 has all three terms uniquely together to emphasise the whole self, whereas St Paul generally uses two terms elsewhere.

33 R. J. Berry, *God and the Biologist* (Apollos, 1996), p.30. Chimps

do of course share a rudimentary consciousness, it is thought, somewhat beyond stimulus/response (see Question 31). Chimps cannot talk and even with training by humans a ceiling of development is apparently rapidly reached.

34 Geneticists are making some headway in trying to insert genetic material to produce healthy cells that are not subsequently naturally displaced by faulty ones (see Question 43).

35 Richard Dawkins, *River out of Eden* (Phoenix, 1995), p.155.

36 The stronger form says culture is just a means to the end of genes reproducing themselves (see Question 28).

37 John Bowker (with Quinton Deeley), *Is God a Virus?* (SPCK, 1995). Part one of the book is a rebuttal of sociobiological speculation on human society.

38 Their number limitations run to *one, two, lots* ... it appears. Whether they would recognise the concept of counting is doubtful.

39 Blaise Pascal, *Pensées* (frag. 347, 1659).

40 Susan A. Greenfield, *Journey to the Centers of the Mind* (Freeman, 1995), p.29. Professor Greenfield notes an analogy with the light on an iron registering when it is switched on, but not itself mediating the power.

41 Details can be found on the Internet at http://www.columbia.edu/cu/psychology/primatecognitionlab/

42 By which he meant a system of beliefs designed to gratify us. It might or might not be false, though Freud held no Christian beliefs. The use of such a pejorative word (rather like the word 'myth') often accompanies an underlying anti-faith agenda.

43 Fraser Watts (ed.), *Science Meets Faith* (SPCK, 1998), pp.69ff.

44 Thomas Nagel, *The View from Nowhere* (Oxford University Press, 1986), p.8.

45 John Searle, *The Rediscovery of the Mind* (MIT Press, 1994), p.5.

46 Proponents of strong Artificial Intelligence take the view that all thought is information processing, and minds, like software, can be machine independent. Weak AI followers suggest this may only be partially done, but essentially this is the position most taken. Our brains often behave in a computational fashion.

47 John Puddefoot, *God and the Mind Machine* (SPCK, 1996).

48 Development of intelligent machines is currently investigating the area of mimicking the voracious behaviour of infants. In this way we recreate rather than create. Consciousness may develop rudimentarily in electronics as it did biochemically, but probably not for many decades. Our first robot creatures may be more like our beloved pets than the dangerous adult-like killers favoured by sci-fi movies! See http://www.ai.mit.edu for examples.

49 Dorothee Soelle, quoted in Peter Baelz, *Prayer and Providence* (SCM, 1968), p.126.

50 Paraphrase from David Hume, *An Enquiry Concerning Human Understanding* (1748).

51 Michael E. McCullough, *Journal of Psychology and Theology*, vol. 23.1, 1995, pp.15–29.

52 A prayer diary might be an example of this. Prayers not responded to in positive ways might also indicate other areas to be addressed (2 Samuel 12:16ff.), or require perseverance by the person praying or the person being prayed for, as in any relationship.

53 Randolph C. Byrd, *Southern Medical Journal*, vol. 81, 1988, pp.826–829. Reduced instances of subsequent heart failure episodes, pneumonia, and antibiotic use were among the benefits recorded.

54 Reproduction via an unfertilised egg is called parthenogenesis from this Greek word.

55 If the same child is being referred to, as seems very possible.

56 Article in *The Independent*, Christmas Eve, 1993, and 'The Virgin Birth of Christ', *Science and Christian Belief*, vol. 8.2, 1996, pp.101–110, and a subsequent debate in vol. 9.1.

57 One would be that the woman carried an unexpressed Y (male) chromosome, and was otherwise physically normal, and could conceive. If the egg developed parthenogenetically and the Y chromosome switched on, a virgin birth of a male child could occur.

58 N. T. Wright, *The New Testament and the People of God* (SPCK, 1992), p.335. His book *Who Was Jesus?* (SPCK, 1992) provides an excellent selection of arguments against recent writers like

A. N. Wilson and John Spong.

59 Oliver O'Donovan, *Resurrection and Moral Order* (IVP, 1986), chapter 1.

60 Dr Alan Coleman, co-researcher in producing a cloned sheep, writes about the unacceptability of cloning people. A person should never be the 'product of an assembly line', he says. 'Why cloning would be inhuman', *The Times* 15th June 1998.

61 An example of this is the personal assessment by the Prince of Wales in *The Daily Telegraph*, 9th June 1998.

62 1871. Quoted in Ian G. Barbour, *Religion and Science* (SCM Press, 1998), p.60.

63 Richard Leakey, *The Sixth Extinction* (Phoenix, 1997), p.46. The others are at around 440, 365, 235 and 210 million years ago. Several causes are possible (including asteroid or comet hits), and the reasons behind them are not fully understood, but climate change plays a significant role.

64 Athanasius, *On the Incarnation*, section 54, written around AD 335/6.

65 Stephen May in his analysis of science fiction explores this desire to become god-like: *Stardust and Ashes – Science Fiction in Christian Perspective* (SPCK, 1998). A hopeful and positive forecast is provided by Michio Kaku, *Visions*, (Oxford University Press, 1998), ch.8.

66 Frank J. Tipler, *The Physics of Immortality* (Macmillan, 1994).

67 Lawrence M. Krauss, *The Physics of Star Trek* (Flamingo, 1996), p.77.

68 Michael J. Reiss and Roger Straughan, *Improving Nature?* (Cambridge University Press, 1996), ch. 7. This clear book gives many examples of the different categories of genetic manipulation.

69 Roslin's web site is http://www2.ri.bbsrc.ac.uk. Future projects and ethical issues are discussed. Links to the discussion with the Church of Scotland's Society, Religion and Technology Project are given.

70 In the UK and the USA, research on human embryos after fourteen days is not permitted. At eighteen days a recognisable nerve system begins to form.

71 A good starting web site is http://www.dti.gov.uk/hgac for UK contributions and through this to the American Christian debate. The contribution of the Prince of Wales to the GM debate is at http://www.princeofwales.gov.uk/forum. For a contrary view see the web site of the International Food Information Council at http://ificinfo.health.org/brochure/biobenef.html.

72 Michael Green, *After Alpha* (Kingway, 1998), p.246.

73 Quoted in Rob Frost and David Wilkinson, *Thinking Clearly about God and Science* (Monarch, 1997), p.204.

For Further Reading

Many books are being published in this expanding field, some better than others. If you would like to carry on exploring this subject, here are a few books that go into more depth.

R. J. (Sam) Berry, *God and the Biologist* (Apollos (IVP), 1996).

Malcolm Jeeves, *Mind Fields* (Apollos (IVP), 1994).

Donald M. Mackay, *The Clockwork Image* (IVP Christian Classics, 1997).

Gilbert Meilaender, *Bioethics – a Primer for Christians* (Paternoster, 1996).

John Polkinghorne, *Quarks, Chaos and Christianity* (Triangle, 1994).

Christopher Southgate and others, *God, Humanity and the Cosmos* (T & T Clark, 1999).

Russell Stannard, *Science and Wonders* (Faber and Faber, 1996).

Thomas F. Torrance, *Space, Time and Incarnation* (T&T Clark, 1997 edn) – harder going.

Keith Ward, *God, Faith and the New Millennium*

(Oneworld, 1998).
Fraser Watts (ed.), *Science Meets Faith* (SPCK, 1998).
David Wilkinson and Rob Frost, *Thinking Clearly about God and Science* (Monarch, 1996).